PRAISE FOR *THE OFFICE SURVIVAL GUIDE*

"Street smarts and corporate savvy in one professional. A rare find."
—Walter B. Wriston, late Chairman and CEO, Citicorp

"Every employee wants to know what are the secrets to getting ahead. Marilyn Puder-York nails it with practical, how-to tips, ideas and solutions. This should be a MUST read whether you are 26 or 46."
—Cathleen Black, President of Hearst Magazines

"I found this book to be right on target. Marilyn Puder-York understands the complex problems that employees face in difficult work situations. Everyone working in an organization should read this book."
—Arun Sinha, Chief Marketing Officer, Pitney Bowes

"Marilyn Puder-York has made an extremely positive impact on our ability to retain talented people in our organization. Her book extends her considerable talents to a broader audience and will no doubt help retain talent in many organizations."
—Douglas Stern, President/CEO, United Media

"At last! Marilyn Puder-York has put her wisdom in writing. With *The Office Survival Guide*, you will gain the crucial insights and advice you need to manage yourself and others. Marilyn has worked with the Five O'Clock Club clients for years and has always received rave reviews for her crisp understanding and personable advice. What can be more important to your career success than learning how to manage your boss, peers and subordinates? Marilyn shows you how."
—Kate Wendleton, President, The Five O'Clock Club

"Marilyn Puder-York shares her 30 years of experience as a psychologist and executive coach in a wonderfully readable and applicable approach to surviving in the modern office. Whether you're the boss, middle management, or the newest assistant, you'll benefit from her wisdom and understanding of how to manage the trickiest workplace situations."
—Dorothy W. Cantor, Psy.D., former president,
American Psychological Association, and author of
What Do You Want To Do When You Grow Up?

"This book is like Dr. Marilyn Puder-York herself—warm, wise, down-to-earth, practical and eminently useful. She cuts through psychological jargon to lead leaders though their pasts to a more powerful grasp of the present they operate in. Anyone who aspires to be an effective leader can benefit from the tools she provides."

—Amanda Bennett, Executive Vice President
and Editor, *The Philadelphia Inquirer*,
and Pulitzer Prize winning editor and author

"Marilyn Puder-York is at ease with her subject. This thoughtful, easy-to-read book will help so many people cope more effectively with tough work situations. I recommend it highly!"

—Marc Porter, President, Christie's Americas

"This book is awesome and a gem! It is smart reading for all levels of employees in any organization."

—J. Charles Cardona, Vice Chairman, Dreyfus Corporation

"A real find!! Sound and powerful advice for surviving office difficulties. Required reading for employees everywhere."

—Maggie Gagliardi, Senior Vice President,
Human Resources, American Express Company

"In her eminently readable book, Marilyn Puder-York captures the wisdom she imparts to her corporate clients every day. Her sound and practical advice is right on and very useful in today's business environment."

—Tom Bernardin, CEO, Leo Burnett Worldwide, Inc.

"I believe it is critically important for all parties (employees and bosses) in today's pressured business environment to feel that they share responsibility for creating a constructive, healthy workplace and to have the tools to manage themselves and others around them. This is a 'must read' for anyone who shares this perspective; and it is especially critical for HR practitioners who must deal with these issues personally, plus have the responsibility for coaching everyone involved."

—Jean M. Broom, Senior Vice President, ITOCHU
International, Inc., Board Member of the HR Planning Society,
and Co-President of the NY HR Planning Society

"*The Office Survival Guide* provides a unique menu of solutions to understand as well as navigate the challenges of difficult people and situations at work."

—Phebe Farrow Port, Vice President, Corporate Management
Strategies, The Estée Lauder Companies

"Marilyn Puder-York skillfully tackles the complicated topics by presenting the psychological aspects of individual behavior and the political aspects of the work environment in a manner that is understandable and useable. Read this book and you will function more powerfully!"

—Marie C. Wilson, President, The White House Project/
Women's Leadership Fund and author, *Closing the Leadership Gap*

The Office Survival Guide

Surefire Techniques for Dealing with Challenging People and Situations

Marilyn Puder-York, Ph.D.
with
Andrea Thompson

McGraw-Hill
New York Chicago San Francisco Lisbon
London Madrid Mexico City Milan New Delhi
San Juan Seoul Singapore Sydney Toronto

The **McGraw·Hill** Companies

1 2 3 4 5 6 7 8 9 0 DOC/DOC 0 9 8 7 6 5

ISBN 0-07-146203-1

This publication is designed to provide accurate and authoritative information in regard to the subject matter covered. It is sold with the understanding that neither the author nor the publisher is engaged in rendering legal, accounting, or other professional service. If legal advice or other expert assistance is required, the services of a competent professional person should be sought.
—From a Declaration of Principles jointly adopted by Committee of the American Bar Association and a Committee of Publishers.

McGraw-Hill books are available at special quantity discounts to use as premiums and sales promotions, or for use in corporate training programs. For more information, please write to the Director of Special Sales, McGraw-Hill Professional, Two Penn Plaza, New York, NY 10121-2298. Or contact your local bookstore.

 This book is printed on recycled, acid-free paper containing a minimum of 50% recycled, de-inked fiber.

Library of Congress Cataloging-in-Publication Data

Puder-York, Marilyn.
   The office survival guide : surefire techniques for dealing with challenging people and situations / by Marilyn Puder-York, with Andrea Thompson.
       p.   cm.
   ISBN 0-07-146203-1 (alk. paper)
   1. Psychology, Industrial.   2. Interpersonal relations.   3. Organizational behavior.
I. Thompson, Andrea (Andrea B.)   II. Title.

HF5548.8.P8185 2006
650.1—dc22   2005024629

To the two loves of my life—my husband, Christopher C. York, and my daughter, Sarah Jaclyn York.

To the memories of two great business leaders who possessed character and humanity—the late Walter B. Wriston and the late William I. Spencer. Together, they fostered a corporate environment in which the talented not only survived, but flourished.

Contents

Preface

The Office Survival Guide is going to show you how to get along a lot better with just about anybody in your organization. It is going to outline ways you can handle the most unpleasant, worrisome, crazy-making job situations you're likely to face—what I call the top 10 trickiest workplace events—and come out with your sanity and integrity intact, not to mention your job. We will be talking about triggers and "blind spots," which are the personal, highly individual reactions in the office that can all too easily *stop* you from getting along better with anybody and dealing successfully with those tough situations.

We all have them, blind spots. Let me tell you a little about my background, my experience, and how I came to write this book. It has something to do with my own blind spots.

As a Ph.D. clinical psychologist, I migrated from the beginning of my career in mental health services to the world of business. For close to 30 years, most recently as an executive coach hired by some of the top Fortune 500 companies, I have helped hard-working, talented individuals deal with their internal issues and their reactions to work, and find the best accommodation between the two.

Before opening my own practice, I applied my skills working in city government, in the nonprofit sector, on Wall Street as a private practitioner counseling executives, and for 10 years as corporate vice president and head of the internal employee assistance program in a Fortune 100 financial company. During my tenure at that company, our in-house efforts expanded to provide not only support with health and mental health issues, including drug and alcohol counseling, but stress management, family/worklife balance counseling, preretirement preparation, and executive coaching. I supervised a staff; we consulted with more than 1,000 people a year.

As a corporate employee, I observed how individual behavior is shaped by the impact of an organization on personal dynamics. I saw men and women doing themselves real damage by reacting unwisely or inappropriately to one or another workplace event. I came to understand this intimately, not abstractly. In fact, the process that I lead my clients through today, and that I am going to present to you in the following chapters, developed in large part from the insight I gained—painfully at the time—into my own blind spots. A bit of personal history:

My family background included growing up as an only child with a widowed mother who needed (and wanted) a great deal of emotional and practical support from me—I was assigned the role of "rescuing" her in a very real sense. So, early on, I came to believe that adults often required my help. Several teachers along the way, in addition, tended to confide in me about school issues and seek my advice, adding to my perception that authority figures turned to me at critical junctures. This, then, was the dynamic I brought into corporate life heading up a large employee assistance program. My self-esteem was closely attached to my ability to solve problems and rescue people in adverse situations.

There came a day when I was informed that, for budgetary and other reasons, I had to abolish my department. This was a business decision, wise or not, that obviously my superiors had the power to make. They were not asking me to behave unethically; they were saying, dismantle what you developed because it no longer fits corporate plans. I didn't see things that way. Here's what I saw instead: These awful people are taking away my role as a rescuer and are destroying my "family;" I will fight them! This was my blind spot. My response was one of anger; I rebelled; I jumped into action, arguing all the reasons I believed they were making a huge mistake. To a large degree, my unwise responses made it necessary for me to leave the company.

By reacting emotionally to a business decision that I didn't agree with, I did myself damage. Had I been able to control my emotions, appreciate the fact that I was dealing not with a mother or father or family but with a corporation, a political entity, I almost surely would have been able to negotiate a happier outcome to a tricky situation.

But here is the positive fallout: My painful experience turned out to be a powerful turning point, one that taught me crucial lessons. I might even say that as a professional, it was the best thing to happen to me. If I had had the kind of support system that *The Office Survival Guide* will offer you, I would not have allowed my blind spots to cloud my judgment and shape my actions.

An added personal note: On September 11, 2001, I was the resident of a building directly across the street from the World Trade Center and witnessed the events of that day firsthand. To a very large degree, that experience served as a catalyst and an impetus to my writing this book. I felt newly motivated to act on the suggestions I had been hearing from many of my colleagues and clients over the years, to share some of my insight and wisdom with more people and in a broader way. I found myself rising to the level of making a commitment to write, because I believed many people need help and support, especially during an extended era of increased anxiety.

A word about what *The Office Survival Guide* is not and won't do:

A number of factors can have an impact on how people respond to situations in day-to-day office life, including an individual's gender, race, culture, and socialization. Many academic studies have explored those factors, but I am not addressing such issues here. This isn't intended to be a research-based survey of organizational development or a textbook on clinical psychology in the workplace. It is a practical, straightforward, anecdotal guide to managing mental well-being and tough job situations. The strategies and understanding that I'm trying to communicate come from, yes, my training as a psychologist, but more importantly, from my streetwise experience talking and listening to hundreds of employees over many years.

That experience has taught me, frankly, that the real behaviors of real people on the job don't always match what the studies sometimes suggest. For example, I have found that often women react the way men are "supposed to" react, and vice versa. What I'm presenting here are general rules that I believe apply to every person, regardless of gender and cultural differences. They derive from my observations as I have helped individuals survive and thrive in their jobs, sometimes under enormous stress.

Although my suggestions are generic and applicable to anyone, they are pointed primarily toward those who work in organizations that employ more than five people and are somewhat hierarchal in nature—that is, an office environment that includes bosses, peers or coworkers, and subordinates. An entrepreneur, a consultant, or an individual contributor who's selling her expertise to multiple corporations might not find as much direct support or relevance.

I talk about the "top 10" trickiest workplace situations. In my experience, these are the dilemmas that pop up again and again. Other than loss of a job, they turn out to be the most significant and to trigger the most intense emotional reactions from the most people. However, my top 10 doesn't necessarily constitute an exhaustive list, and you might have other "bad day in the office" experiences to relate. It's an unlimited world of stressful situations out there! Even so, you'll find here a useful process to begin thinking about how to resolve your particular office difficulty, whatever it might be.

In the chapters that follow, I refer to John and Joe, Michelle and Amy, and others. They are composites I have constructed to give a voice and a face to the dynamics I am describing. In the course of coaching hundreds of individuals and hearing their stories about on-the-job problems, common themes have emerged and those have determined the shape of this book. However, names and specific details in the scenarios I present do not correspond to real individuals with whom I've worked.

In my consulting practice, my job as an executive coach has been to mediate between two worlds: the external world of work and the inner world of my clients. I am there to help them respond to a unique environment in the most adaptive ways they can—accurately, ethically, and with full self-awareness. In *The Office Survival Guide*, I hope to do the same for you.

Acknowledgments

I want to thank Patricia Kitchen, the *Newsday* journalist, who very early on in my career understood and appreciated my two-step approach to helping people solve work problems. She encouraged me to write about my ideas. Until I met Lynn Goldberg one month after September 11, 2001, I had resisted Patricia's and my clients' urgings that I write a book. Lynn's encouragement, coming at such a crucial time, finally triggered the spark to initiate writing a book about my work. Thank you, Lynn.

It was only when I met my dedicated and talented cowriter Andrea Thompson that my raw book outline took professional form. Collaborating with Andrea on my book has been a complete joy. Our agent, the enthusiastic Stedman Mays, shepherded the proposal and successfully found our editor Donya Dickerson at McGraw-Hill. She has been consistently accessible for ongoing help throughout the process. I would also like to thank Keith Fox and his expert team of professionals at McGraw-Hill for their interest and support.

While working on the book, I had the support of advisors, colleagues, friends, and family. I especially want to thank Barbara Katersky and Carol Zacharias. Both took time out of their busy schedules to fact check certain sections of the book. For their ongoing support, I also want to thank Lauren Ashwell, Karen Banoff, Jean Broom, Irene Cohen, Kathy D'Amato, Katina Demetra, Janice Reals Ellig, Kim Eves, Leslie Freeman, Carol Glickman, Barri Hammer, Linda Kane, Ann McMahon, Wilfred Sessoms, and Heidi Steiger.

I want to acknowledge Kathy Wriston and Susan Spencer for

carrying forward the legacy of good business practices established by their husbands at Citicorp/Citibank.

Thank you, my Battery Park City (New York) and Old Greenwich (Connecticut) network of working moms who offered sanity checks during times of work/life balance challenges. I want to thank the staff at Gould, McCoy, Chadick, Ellig for consistently being supportive.

I also thank my husband and daughter. They are my safety net and the place I go for unconditional love. My husband has always been my personal mentor and greatest cheerleader, and my daughter is my greatest inspiration and joy. I thank my stepchildren, Susan and Langley Gace and Craig and Mikako York, for designating to me the role of Bubby to their children, a great privilege that I hold dear.

I thank all the Human Resource professionals, senior executives, and mental health professionals I have collaborated with through my career. Finally, I thank all the individual and corporate clients I have coached through my many years of practice. Much of the book has been based on their sharing of experiences. I thank them for sharpening my skills and expanding my knowledge and humanity.

Love to you all.

1

About Tigers and Alley Cats

WORKPLACE TRIGGERS AND HOW TO NAME YOURS

Today's office is all too often not a cozy place. We work in fast-moving, highly politicized companies, where the most Machiavellian employee rather than the most talented just might get the promotion. We're forced to co-exist with others behaving badly (a threatening or impossible boss, an incompetent assistant, a super-competitive coworker). We need to adapt, and ever more quickly, to shakeups and changes.

Chances are, sooner or later you will come up against one or another of these nasty situations, if you're not in the middle of one already. When it happens, most people experience a degree of what I call reactive anxiety—a perfectly normal feeling of stress in response to an abnormal though common event. Some have a harder time than others, mainly because of ancient, highly personal vulnerabilities. For them, tricky situations can turn the workplace toxic.

Here's the good news. You can, absolutely, learn to weather

, or bad stretches at work and come away stronger than ever. In ...is book, I'm going to show you how to:

- Understand the beast (internal or external) you're facing on the job.
- Stop yourself from making a big mistake.
- Figure out your smartest moves.
- Take the actions that will defuse the crisis.
- Adjust your coping skills for future use.

Put it together, and not only will life at the office become more bearable, but you will also manage your career more creatively. You will survive and thrive, practically and psychologically, in today's volatile work world—whether you're a recent graduate just starting out, or someone who is in midcareer hoping to maintain a hard-won position, or an older individual determined to hang on until retirement.

My approach derives from two premises, or what I call the two realities: Know your blind spots. Know your organization and those who work in it.

THE TIGER OR THE ALLEY CAT: TWO REALITIES

The first reality is internal, unique to each and every one of us. Internal reality consists of the rational or not so rational patterns of thoughts, feelings, and actions with which you confront a difficult situation. The first reality reveals your blind spots, which in all likelihood have been lurking there for most of your life. Blind spots might result from past traumas, painful childhood experiences, or difficult family relation-ships; over time, they become survival strategies, learned ways of gaining security and avoiding anxiety. Or, blind spots might be char-acteristics of a personality style, the downside as opposed to the strengths of what you're all about. Blind spots might refer back to childhood, but they're not necessarily dysfunctional. Recognize them, manage them, and they won't defeat you.

The second reality is external. External reality consists of all the forces at play that make up the context of your life, that you cannot control directly, and that trigger responses from you. When external reality stirs up powerful emotions, those responses can be misguided and possibly damaging.

When working with my clients, I like to use the analogy of the tiger and the alley cat. Let's say that at age five you were badly frightened at the zoo by a tiger that growled and pawed at you from its cage. You dreamt about the tiger for months, waking up in the middle of the night with a scream. Years passed; you forgot about the scary tiger; you stopped having tiger dreams.

Let's say you are now 35 and taking a stroll one night, when in the beam of a car's headlights you see an exaggerated feline shadow. The shadow creature is huge. You experience terror. You gasp for breath and freeze, reaching for a stick to drive the beast back. What hops onto the sidewalk in front of you, however, is a harmless alley cat that doesn't give you a glance.

If it had been a tiger, terror would have been a rational feeling and grabbing a stick might have been a smart thing to do. But see how you assumed without really knowing? There is your blind spot. You flipped into terror mode based on ancient projections, and reacted before having accurate information.

THE ART OF REALITY TESTING

In the work environment, the trigger event will be anything difficult or different. Clearly, if all is running smoothly and pretty much the way it always has, you probably feel calm and confident. If, however, one of those tricky situations arises, you might be less effective in handling the unpleasantness than you need to be, based on your particular vulnerabilities.

For example: Your boss switches gears three-quarters into the report you've been working on, and announces that what you've come up with is not what she wanted at all. What then? Do you launch an e-mail to the boss that afternoon, full of outrage and accusations? Do you slink back to your office feeling embarrassed, wounded, and worried, not making points or asking questions that should be asked? Do you smile through gritted teeth and go along with the new directives, only to sabotage them at your earliest convenience? Clearly, none of these reactions is in your best interests.

Before it is possible to craft a good solution to a bad situation, you must put the reality of the moment to the test.

Slow down knee-jerk reactions; in other words, analyze the environment, and decide if you're facing a tiger or an alley cat. Grasp the two realities, and you can weather difficult situations successfully, or at least without paying a high price. In the best-case outcome, you will shape responses that are almost ideal—politically correct, adaptive to the context, productive for your own needs and goals, and nondestructive to others, basically a win-win situation.

So let us begin.

The following 10 chapters describe what I have learned as being the most challenging, most high-stress work-related situations people find themselves in (other than actually losing a job). Invariably, they trigger particular blind spots in the average person—with mild to moderate to ferociously damaging effects, depending largely on individual vulnerabilities. Without question, these events can be career killers if they're not managed wisely.

For each scenario, I will explain the common emotions and behaviors the situation tends to provoke and the most significant or likely external factors in operation. Then we will consider appropriate solutions.

Of course, target your particular problem or trigger situation—new management coming in and changing all the rules, perhaps, or a boss overloading you with impossible assignments. But even better: Do read the whole book, even those chapters that seem not to pertain to your office life at the moment. Each chapter builds on the whole. You will learn throughout and enlarge your repertoire of coping skills and strategies.

THE LARGER GOAL, THE BIGGER PAYOFF

Yes, the work world of today is often an uneasy environment, one that is in part being shaped by the implosion of companies, upsetting acquisitions and mergers, rapidly changing technology, corporate scandals, and more. From coaching and counseling hundreds of talented men and women and hearing their stories, I have found that many are experiencing psychic pain from the shock waves of change that are transforming their work lives.

But in addition: Our society, our world, is in the midst of a profound disruption from multiple triggers—psychological and physical devastation from terrorist activities and war, and deepening concerns about personal economic well-being. People are fearful, unsettled, living with a sense of irrationality and lack of personal control. All such pressures increase levels of chronic anxiety, and chronic anxiety can so easily lead to dysfunction, on the job and elsewhere.

What I hope this book will do for you: Now, more than ever, the better able we are as individuals to control our own blind spots and reactions to them, within the small worlds each of us travels in, the better geared we will be to handle those bigger triggers over which, frankly, we have little or no control. When you understand yourself a bit better and learn more about adapting to difficult office situations, you reduce anxiety and fearfulness on a day-to-day level at work.

And when you tame the tigers in your work environment, you'll manage the rest of life with greater confidence, energy, and strength.

My focus is on workplace triggers, but my hope is that in the process of learning how to respond rationally to nasty and irrational situations on the job, you will also gain a dynamic way of looking at the other demands you meet each day. Triggers are everywhere, after all—in our marriages, in our parenting roles. In the idea of internal and external realities, of tigers and alley cats, you'll discover a framework that helps you manage your responses to all the triggers that are part of our complex and busy modern lives.

PART 1

SURVIVING PEOPLE

A FEW FIRST THOUGHTS

The trigger situations in the business world that cause the most stress are the difficult behaviors of significant others in a work environment. By significant others, I'm talking about the boss, the peer/coworker, and the subordinate/assistant. With these individuals, the people you have to get along with on a daily basis, you are right in the middle of relationship issues, with all the vexations they involve.

Of course, "difficult" behaviors and the psychological effects they produce are as variable as are people. What you find disturbing, annoying, infuriating, or impossible might be taken in relative stride by the guy who works down the hall from you. However, several consistent patterns across the board seem to be directly related to the degree or the intensity of stress caused by the human relationships in your job life:

- The more real power the significant other wields, the more stress you're likely to experience from her behaviors. On average, therefore, most people are more bothered by a difficult boss than by a difficult secretary.

- The more power you *give* the individual who is behaving badly, the more stress you're likely to feel. Typically, we empower those people who linger in our psychological baggage. If, for example, you're still battling unresolved sibling rivalry issues, you might very well find the competitive co-worker the hardest to deal with in a constructive way.

- The more *ongoing* the difficult behavior, the more intense the stress. A basically fair and consistent boss who occasionally acts in an off-the-wall or unreasonable manner will probably cause less intense anxiety than one who is day-in and day-out impossible.

- The more the behavior is experienced as abusive, threatening, or humiliating, regardless of the chain of command levels, the higher the stress.

- The more you feel trapped, unable to escape, the more miserable it becomes going into the office each morning. In the old days, leaving for another job or organization—or even thinking about doing so—might have been a fine coping strategy. In today's world, we're only too aware that our options might be skimpy or nonexistent.

- The more supportive the organization is, in general, the less intense your stress. You're likely to find your people problem easier to handle, that is, if you know you have available to you organizational support systems,

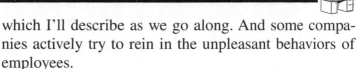

which I'll describe as we go along. And some companies actively try to rein in the unpleasant behaviors of employees.

Beyond these factors, other patterns emerge depending on the particular significant relationship: you and your boss, you and your peer/coworker, you and your subordinate. In the following three chapters, we look at just what those are, why they cause such pressure, and how they can be handled with smarts, style, empathy, and constructive action. Most important: I will show you how to manage your significant other behaving badly in a way that leaves you in a stronger, healthier, happier position than when you started.

2

The Difficult Boss

HOW TO SOOTHE YOUR SUPERIOR
AND PROTECT YOURSELF

We might come up with a thousand stories about difficult bosses: the boss who gives you a cheery "hi" one day and looks right through you the next, the one who never has a good word for a job well done, the one who resorts to sarcasm to convey his expectations, the one who shouts and screams to express her expectations, and on and on. Broadly speaking, this individual's actions in the moment are unpleasant and/or unreasonable, given his position and given the behavior of the employee on the receiving end. In this chapter, we narrow the field to focus on two scenarios:

- Hostile behavior from the boss—and how employee Carl coped
- Seductive behavior from the boss—and how employee Emily coped

11

Carl's and Emily's dilemmas might not be identical to one you face, or will face at some point along the way. The facts might be something else entirely; your difficult boss behaves in another way or operates within a very different context. *However*, the process— exploring what's going on internally and externally, and what that suggests in terms of appropriate, self-protective strategies on your part—is the same.

In my experience, of all the trigger situations in the workplace, the difficult boss is probably the toughest to handle for the majority of individuals. Which is perhaps not so surprising, because it centers on a man or woman who just might hold the key to your future and the purse strings to your present life—and a man or a woman who triggers dad or mom in your emotions.

So read about the experiences of Carl and Emily, and learn how to deal with the difficult boss, in all of his or her manifestations.

Carl's story: what happened to him one day on the job

Carl, an up-and-coming 35-year-old executive in an investment bank, arrived for work one Tuesday morning confidently anticipating a meeting with his boss and two of his boss's superiors. All four, plus several associates, would be discussing the restructuring plan Carl had been preparing for the previous two months. Carl was no dummy; an MBA, with seven years of corporate experience, he knew the ropes. He'd sent his boss regular interim reports and shown him an outline of the proposal just the previous Friday. His boss had nodded his approval. All systems, it seemed, were go. And this particular project, Carl believed, represented an outstanding opportunity for his next promotion.

The boss's comments at the meeting, however, not only dashed Carl's hopes of a pat on the back and a better job title, but turned off the green light entirely to move forward on the plans. The boss ripped into his report, calling it "juvenile" and "totally off target." "It all had to go back to the drawing board," he said, "and maybe some other people with fresher ideas should be brought in on it."

Carl was shocked. He felt demeaned in front of senior management and several co-workers, and blamed for a "failure" he could not have anticipated. He was also perplexed. Where was this coming from? What had he done wrong? Was the boss angry with him in general? Aware that his face was turning red, Carl sat through the rest of the meeting saying little.

His reaction was far from unusual. When a boss does a number like this, almost always an employee will be flooded with uncomfortable emotions. He might become angry and ready to go on the attack: *I'm going to send him an e-mail and really let him have it with both barrels.* He might become depressed: *I feel so terrible, I can't face anybody; maybe I'm in the wrong line of work.*

Would that there were an easy solution to Carl's dilemma. The picture becomes clearer and the fog of swirling emotions lifts only after thinking through the internal and external realities of what was going on in that conference room that morning.

First, Carl needed to become aware of his blind spots—vulnerabilities that typically prompted him to react in a certain way when under stress. Only within the context of self-knowledge would he be able to figure out how to handle his irrational boss.

The internal reality piece: a diagnostic questionnaire

Bosses tend to push our buttons in a particular way. The common patterns this powerful workplace trigger stirs up—our programmed reactions—are generally an extension of the role we played as children in response to our parents.

In other words, your superior is likely to provoke in you the experience of being parented: how your mother or father treated you and how you felt about that treatment. Faced with an angry, unexpected outburst from a boss, what's your instinctive reaction?

Consider:

• When an authority figure gets angry, do I get angry right back?

Suppose you had a punitive or harshly critical father, and you learned to meet his bullying by being aggressive, provocative, and argumentative. You gave as good as you got. Your automatic response to this authoritarian parent, the response that helped you cope best, was to shout back.

• Do I want to disappear?

When your parent bullied, blew up in rage or was clearly disappointed in you, you felt frightened. You became silent, kept a low profile, and stayed out of his way until your fear and wish to escape abated or until he calmed down.

• Am I disgusted and quietly rebellious?

You viewed your authoritarian parent as something of a jerk and were annoyed that you were obliged to listen to him. You acted the part of the good child, pretended to do what you were told, and disobeyed him in other ways.

If you had a bullying father or mother and now you're faced with a bullying boss, doesn't it make sense that your internal reaction to the current bully in your life is the same as it was way back when?

• Am I puzzled, and assume I must be in the wrong?

Maybe father or mother wasn't a bullying type at all, but a fair, rational, and generally wise individual on whom you relied for not only loving support and praise, but constructive feedback—a needed reality check from time to time. So an angry flare-up on his or her part meant you'd fallen way below expectations in some way.

Here's what Carl figured out: "When I do a good job, I expect other people to realize that and tell me so. That's the way life should go—you do something well, and you're acknowledged for it. That's only fair. So when I didn't get acknowledged by my boss— worse, when I got blasted out of the water—I was totally confused. I thought it must be me, for some reason."

Carl's life story to date had set him up for his particular blind spot, which, paradoxically, might be considered a rather positive one. He had been parented well, enjoying a peaceful childhood with a loving and encouraging mother and father, and a good relationship with his two brothers. All three siblings were raised with a sense of meritocracy: work hard, perform well, and your successes will be applauded. And Carl did work hard and did perform well, attending an excellent college and graduate school and earning the praise of teachers and professors along the way. Adding to this sunny picture: When Carl entered the job world, he had the good fortune to work with two bosses in succession who recognized his talents, rewarded his efforts, and treated him fairly. Almost all of his experiences with authority figures, in other words, had been affirming and positive— until his recent troubles with his current boss.

We could say that Carl was more than a little naive. He lacked street smarts. Because nothing in his background had prepared him to view this latest authority figure in his life with detachment, he took his boss's attack personally: *What did I do wrong here? Have I done something to hurt his feelings, maybe yesterday or last week? Is he mad at me?* In Carl's understanding of how the world works, there was also a bit of an expectation that a boss was there to serve him (not the other way around): *If I work well, my boss should make me feel good, as my parents did.*

What's key to remember in a scene such as the one Carl went through is this: Though on a certain level you might feel like a child, you are not. And your boss isn't your parent. Granted, he does hold an amount of real power over you, simply by virtue of being your boss. However, you are a paid employee and as such you have your own degree of adult power. To use it, you must detach from and control those now-inappropriate old feelings.

If your blind spot is, "I had a rotten father and now I have a rotten boss and I want to strangle the guy," learn to manage your anger.

If your blind spot is, "I had a rotten father and I always felt like a victim and I tried to hide from him," learn to manage your pattern of withdrawing.

If your blind spot is, "I had a rotten father and I pretended to go along but I got back at him in other ways," learn to manage your temptation to act on thoughts of revenge or sabotage.

If your blind spot is, "I expected my parent to praise me for a job well done and I wasn't praised, so it must be about me," learn not to jump on assumptions of personal failure.

Feelings are real; they will not be banished. Act on those emotions and assume they're pointing you in a good direction, however, and you're more than likely to behave in ways that are maladaptive to the event. Feelings should be recognized and labeled, and then buffered and controlled, in whatever healthful way works best.

Again, Carl was no dummy. He recognized it would be wise to detach a bit emotionally, and allow himself time to think things through. A self-confessed gym nut, Carl increased his workouts for the next couple of days, letting his emotions settle down. Intellectually, he knew his work on the project was first-rate. The boss's criticism had been undeserved, and also expressed in a hostile manner. Maybe, Carl wondered, something was going on with the boss that he didn't know about. And before he could determine a plan of action, he needed to spend time figuring out what that might be.

In other words, what external realities could be uncovered?

Before we see how Carl can handle his tricky situation, a few words about bosses in general:

The difficult boss: three behavioral profiles

In the scenarios you'll read throughout this book, the boss appears again and again among the dramatis personae. Often, he's the lead character, the key to a satisfactory outcome to a bad dilemma you're having involving work assignments and expectations, clashes with colleagues, or other issues. Situational triggers vary, but resolving a problem in so many cases means approaching the boss in some way.

If you are working for an agreeable, rational, intelligent and empathetic individual, consider yourself extremely lucky. Sooner or later, however, you are likely to run up against the difficult boss, or the boss behaving in a way that makes it difficult for you to do your job. He must be addressed carefully. It's called managing up, and doing so successfully—in a problem solving manner, diffusing defensiveness and conflict, motivating this person to deal with a problematic issue or modify behavior—can make all the difference to your job life and career. At the same time, psychologically astute managing up doesn't always work with certain types at certain stages of the game.

So, how do you deconstruct your particular difficult boss, in order to determine how best to interact with him or her?

Over my years as a coach, I have observed three general categories of difficult bosses, those who exhibit irrational behavior occasionally or constantly. They are:

- ### *The overstressed good guy*
  He's been pushed by unaccustomed pressures in the environment—at work or in his personal life—and can sometimes

act in ways that are not typical of him. The stress he's feeling might show up in a low tolerance for frustration, temper tantrums, insane demands, dumb decisions, or inconsistency. Under normal circumstances, however, this boss is a good guy. When not under unusual pressures, he can be counted on for fair treatment.

• *The politician/constructive narcissist*

He's a generally self-absorbed and selfish individual. This boss tends to manage up (with *his* bosses) and horizontally very nicely, but shows little empathy or good communication skills downward. Although his behavior might appear off-the-wall, offensive, exploitative, or irrational to subordinates, he—like the good guy—is seldom intentionally destructive.

• *The bad guy/destructive narcissist*

Think of the ogre straight out of Grimm's Fairy Tales. In his drive for personal success and recognition, he uses employees as tools, even playthings. This individual might lie with impunity, blame others, steal ideas, or devalue co-workers in order to get ahead.

With these last two—the politician and the bad guy—it's all about him or her.

If you have been working with your boss for a while, you probably have some idea of which category he occupies. If you don't have much of a track record with this individual, you might not have had enough contact to be sure just who or what you're dealing with. In that case especially, due diligence will fill you in on what you probably need to know.

Due diligence—or exploring the external reality of the situation—is what I put my clients through, in order to place the boss accurately somewhere within the three profiles. When I meet with a client, it is not uncommon for this smart professional to start out by saying, "I have this horrible boss, this awful thing just happened, she's crazy, she's making me crazy, I don't know how I'm going to handle this!" Before we can come up with sensible ideas on that score, I ask a raft of questions to try to get a sense of who the boss is and why she's acting the way she's acting. Is she, in fact, crazy? A benign bully? A pawn of company politics?

Although not an exhaustive list, the questions below are a good way to frame your own due diligence, whenever you have to approach the boss. And you will see the themes introduced here recurring in the various trigger situations we cover in the remaining chapters.

The external reality piece: a diagnostic questionnaire

Remember this: Your assessment of your boss is a factual inquiry, a process of data collection, not a subjective opinion survey of your co-workers. Do not, in other words, expect to find out all the genuinely useful information you need by swapping horror stories around the water cooler.

Ask yourself:

- **Does the boss's behavior reflect a long-term pattern?**
  Has he acted in similarly irrational ways previously, or is this new, out-of-the-blue behavior? The newer, the better. If your boss doesn't regularly fly off the handle, switch gears, or do other unpleasant numbers on his workers, chances are that something out of the ordinary is influencing his mood. He's probably a good guy.

- **Is my boss respected for his accomplishments, known as a visionary with strategic intelligence?**
  If he's a productive, powerful and successful individual, he might be a narcissist, of either stripe. The question then might be: Regardless of his emotional impact on you, will continuing to work for him help you to achieve your own goals, mission or purpose?

- **Is my boss's behavior consistent with or deviant from the management practices of the general organizational culture?**

    Bosses often take their behavioral cues from the upper ranks. Senior people behaving badly (with persistently hostile remarks, for example, or inappropriate socializing with subordinates) create an atmosphere in which negative managerial behavior down is tolerated or even encouraged. If that's the atmosphere you recognize prevails in your office, and your boss is acting the way all the big boys act, you might be dealing with the politician. The more *deviant* your boss's behavior is from the corporate culture, the greater your leverage is in controlling the situation.

- **What is my boss's reputation with my peers?**

    Have they experienced difficult behavior? If so, how did they deal with it? You might be aware of past incidents between the boss and one of your coworkers, or you might want to make some discreet inquiries of a colleague you know and trust, to learn if he's gone through anything similar. But again, remember that you're on a fact-finding mission, not seeking comfort through mutual grousing.

- **What is my boss's turnover rate for subordinates?**

    The lower the better. Clearly, if you discover your boss has run through six assistants in the last two years, others besides you have found him hard to work for, probably because of repeated episodes of irrational behavior.

- **Does my boss accept responsibility when he makes mistakes, or does he try to deny or project blame elsewhere?**

    Bosses, like everyone else, do make mistakes. The ability to say, "My fault; I gave you the wrong figures and we have to redo this estimate," reveals a great deal about a boss's interpersonal strengths, ego issues, or political motivations.

- **Does my boss develop his staff by delegating, increasing responsibility, and rewarding for performance, or does he micromanage, overcontrol, and limit growth?**

   If he consistently fails to delegate, increase responsibility to subordinates, and reward for performance, those behaviors point to the narcissist boss.

- **Does my boss have a history of humiliating, devaluing, or setting up subordinates, either in public or private?**

   Again, you might learn of specific incidents from coworkers. Or if your work life involves fairly regular group get-togethers—the monthly editorial meeting, the Monday morning progress-report session—you have had opportunities to watch your boss in action with staff members. Does he have a tendency to mock, put down, or in other ways cause discomfort to employees who offer ideas he doesn't like?

- **Has the boss been experiencing unusual personal life or work stress?**

   It's not so easy to know, of course, if he's having problems with his delinquent teenage son or he's under financial pressures or his wife is leaving him, but you might hear some news of this sort. What might be more readily apparent is job-related stress—changes in upper management, declining sales, a major project running over schedule, a planned move to new offices, the loss of a valued associate. Any such immediate and extraordinary event suggests the possibility of a good guy boss under pressure.

   A quiet fact-finding mission aimed at better understanding your boss should leave you fairly certain that you have a good handle on who he is and why he acted the way he did. Armed with these insights, you're ready to consider your next moves.

We return to Carl, and see how he might proceed after that disastrous Tuesday morning meeting, depending on what he's decided about his boss. I'll describe three possibilities. They assume three variations in Carl's due diligence findings and in his job history.

Best next steps: dealing with the overstressed good guy

Carl concludes that his boss is a good guy after all.

After working with the man for two years, he's come to know him generally to be a straight shooter. He's observed his boss on more than one occasion delegating responsibilities in a thoughtful and supportive way to subordinates; although he wants results and personal success, the boss seems aware of his need to mentor others. He's well regarded by most of the people who work for him, he's usually willing to listen to new ways of doing things, and he's not mean-spirited. The boss, Carl thinks, must be overstressed for some reason, and in fact, one of Carl's coworkers mentioned that the boss's wife was having some health problems. Not only at the meeting but in several minor incidents of late, Carl's boss seemed not as well focused as usual.

Chances are strong that if Carl finds the appropriate time and directs his communications in a nonattacking but clear and candid manner, his boss might accept responsibility for his unpleasant behavior.

Here are the critical aspects in approaching the good guy who behaves irrationally:

- **Consider the best likely time to voice concerns, objections, or feelings.**

  Clearly, Carl should look for a private and calm moment in which to speak his piece. He should sense whether or not the boss is accessible—he's in his office doing quiet paperwork and not dashing out to a meeting—and in a relatively good mood.

Timing can make all the difference in how well you are heard. If you're in the boss's office and in the middle of a transaction relating to business, don't start bringing in at that point your concerns, objections, or feelings about the incident that rankled you. Raise those issues in a separate meeting in which that will be the focus. On the other hand, if you're in his office discussing business, you've concluded that discussion, he's in a good mood, you can say: "Do you have a few minutes to talk about another matter?" If he says no, let it drop; if he says sure, talk. But always ask permission.

It might be wise not to initiate this talk too quickly. You don't want to add to the pressures an overstressed boss already feels. Should you give him time—a day or two— to come to his senses, realize his inappropriate behavior, and, perhaps, apologize?

- **In the moment, address the issue but maintain a conciliatory tone.**

Carl had kept his mouth shut during that disastrous meeting to discuss the new project. However, if he *had* decided to speak up then and there, he needed to keep his emotions under control and speak in a soothing or friendly manner. For example:

"I'm puzzled. As of two days ago you seemed to be in agreement, but maybe there have been developments since then to change our direction. Thanks for pointing out areas to alter. I'm glad I know the picture now, even if we table this project for the time being."

Keep it simple and to the point, while registering a clear concern.

- **After the moment, maintain a conciliatory tone and explain further.**

Carl can choose to talk to his boss after the unpleasant event and in private, sensing that would be smarter timing.

Because he's decided the boss is basically a good guy, Carl probably would be safe in speaking fairly openly. He might begin with, "I'm puzzled . . . ," as above, then add:

"I know you didn't intend to embarrass me at the meeting, but I would have appreciated a heads-up regarding your negative feedback or change in direction."

It's a smart managing-up move to try to take your boss off the hook by implying or stressing a lack of intentionality on his part.

- **Be empathetic.**

Suspecting the boss was under unusual stress, Carl might add:

"I've noticed you seem under pressure lately, and I'd like to be helpful in some way if I can. Because when you're stressed, it filters down to the staff, and I know that's not your intention."

Often, this kind of communication can ease a boss's anxiety, foster your bond with him, and in an unthreatening manner establish clear boundaries about what you expect. Perhaps your boss could use more support himself. Let him know that you'll provide it, if at all possible, but you would prefer not being treated in such an awkward way. The good guy boss might be able to absorb that information.

Best next steps: dealing with the politician/ constructive narcissist

Carl concludes that his boss is a politician and an egotist.

Although Carl had been working for a couple of months on the project under discussion, and although he'd worked for this particular boss for half a year, that Tuesday morning meeting was the first time he'd been in a group with his boss *and* senior management. And lo and behold, Carl got his first look at how political his boss really was—the man was clearly intent on impressing his superiors with his tough talk and command. Later recalling the exchanges in the room, Carl believed a lot of ego had been on display.

Thinking about two other incidents he'd heard from coworkers, Carl concluded the boss's action at the meeting was not so unusual. This guy was mostly out for himself, and gave little thought to the impact of his behaviors on his subordinates.

Here's what to know about approaching the politician boss:

• Conduct all communication in private.

Speaking out at the meeting would have been a big, big mistake on Carl's part. Regardless of how successfully he kept his emotions in control, he was wise not to communicate his concerns right then and there.

The politician might display a more consistent pattern of irrational behavior than the good guy. In fact, his behavior might represent the cultural norm in senior management ranks. Your boss might have learned to adapt extremely well to a general organizational culture that rewards managing up and encourages selfish managerial behavior down. *His* boss is probably like that too. You might not find your boss a lovable individual, but he's supremely rational in a narrow-minded, essentially self-serving way.

In that situation and with that type of boss, you do *not* want to discuss your difficulties in public. You do *not* want to put this guy on the defensive in front of management (or in front of anyone else, for that matter). He can be approached, but very carefully. Do not risk devaluing him or wounding his ego in any way.

• Find an appropriate time to talk—soon.

Chances are, although his behavior appeared toxic, Carl's boss was not intentionally trying to undermine him. This individual is the nondestructive narcissist, self-absorbed but not out to inflict harm. So if Carl communicates privately and diplomatically, his boss might adjust his behavior. Shortly after the meeting would be the ideal time for Carl to approach for a little talk.

- **Stress your willingness and commitment to be supportive and helpful.**

  Carl might say:

  "I do want to deliver what you require. I now recognize your needs on this project, and I want to assure you of my loyalty and support."

  What this boss wants is for you to please him and serve him. Assure him that that's what you want, too.

- **Point out ways you believe your effectiveness can be enhanced.**

  While Carl needs to underscore his loyalty, he can also add the suggestion that in this case he would have been more effective had he received earlier feedback. He might say:

  "When I presented the plan at the meeting, I assumed I had your support and all the relevant corporate data. Can you let me know what changed since last Friday that seemed to alter the direction we need to go in?"

  Communication with the politician is less direct than with the good guy, and, obviously, more sensitive to his ego concerns. You might not end up in a closer, warmer bond with the egotist, or reduce his tension. Here's what really matters: Motivate him to modify his behavior, without risking the escalation of other interpersonal problems between the two of you.

Best next steps: dealing with the bad guy/ destructive narcissist

Carl concludes that his boss is the destructive narcissist.

In retrospect, Carl realized, his boss's hostile behavior at the meeting shouldn't have come as such a surprise. After working for the man for just over a year, it was becoming ever more apparent to him that the boss regularly either took credit for his subordinate's work or diminished it. Carl hadn't before been on the receiving end of such a dressing-down, but he learned in conversations with several coworkers that they too had been made to look bad in similar circumstances. One such coworker told Carl he'd actually been blamed, wrongly, for failing to submit a required estimate. Carl decided his boss's actions at the meeting were consistent with a pattern of devaluing subordinates while maintaining his power.

Here's what to know about the destructive narcissist:

- **Consider whether or not to tackle this boss at all.**

    After turning over the possibility in his mind, Carl decides there's little to be gained from talking to his boss or seeking an acknowledgment of what had gone on regarding the disastrous presentation.

    Dealing with the destructive narcissist requires the utmost finesse, energy, and strong defenses. The risks might be high when you attempt to engage him, either at the time of irrational behavior or later in a private discussion. He's not interested in seeing your point; he's not open to constructive criticism. Provoke him, and you're bound to lose. So think very carefully about the wisdom of talking to him at all.

- **Continue to appear to be supportive while protecting your ego.**

    As long as Carl remains working for this particular superior, he must try to develop a thick skin—a corporate persona that allows him to survive on the job with his own ego intact. Whenever his blind spots are again triggered by the boss's behavior, he must remember not to personalize what he's hearing or react emotionally in a public manner.

    The fact is, emotional reactions—of anger, deep hurt, humiliation—show vulnerability; you lose your power in whatever situation arises, and transfer the power to your narcissist boss. Aim for self-protection.

• **Talk to a trusted and wise mentor.**

Carl needs to find someone who understands corporate politics inside and out, and who can help guide him through this minefield. Likely possibilities include the individual with a generally acknowledged reputation as discreet, a good person to talk to, one that others have been known to seek out for advice, and/or one who'll be capable of humanely weighing Carl's personal concerns and goals within the context of the organization.

• **Keep track of your exchanges with the boss.**

After that deadly meeting, Carl should begin making notes on his contacts with the boss—considering, wisely, that at some point in the future it might be advisable to consult internal Human Resources (HR) about the difficulties he's been having, and a diary of exchanges with the boss would be useful. (A further discussion of HR appears on page 29.)

• **Consider finding an exit from this boss or the company as soon as possible.**

Carl should be strategizing an exit, either laterally or outside the organization.

Sometimes—not always—the internal HR professional can be helpful in finding a better fit within the company. If Carl believes a meeting with HR might do him some good, he must handle such a talk with great care, and probably present the argument that he'd be "more useful to the company" in another position.

A move to another job or organization isn't always so easy, of course. At least develop the mindset that you *will*, starting immediately, begin exploring other positions. The possibility that the bad guy boss will change his stripes is very, very slight.

However, there's another angle to this story. If your boss is highly accomplished and creates great successes, remaining part of his team might teach you valuable lessons and help you achieve goals you wouldn't be able to reach elsewhere. So it might be important for your career to stick it out for a while. Then, you'll have to cope with the psychological fallout of working for a bad guy by finding your ego and emotional support elsewhere—in other words, by making sure that friendships, hobbies, sports, exercise, or other connections and outlets are a high priority in your life.

HUMAN RESOURCES

• What is human resources and what is it expected to do?

Human resources (HR) is a staff support function found in most organizations. It's sometimes called by other names, such as personnel, staff relations, or employee relations. HR might consist of one or two individuals or, in a large corporation, hundreds.

HR employees are professionals with general or specialized training who support the organization in various ways. Some have a counseling background, MBA degrees, and/or master's degrees in human resource planning. Some HR professionals deal specifically with particular areas of expertise, such as compensation and benefits; others are involved more generally in employee relations, and help with performance reviews, training, succession planning, development, affirmative action, diversity issues, and advice and grievance situations. These are the individuals I'm referring to throughout this book when I suggest approaching HR with your troubling dilemma on the job.

In my experience, HR professionals are high-quality people with excellent motivations. They're eager to be helpful. They are problem solvers, and usually emotionally intelligent about the

continued

impact of work on individuals. At the same time, they will attempt to find a balance between the needs of individual employees and the needs of management. Their challenge is to handle the conflicts that arise in a way that is ethical and honorable, and that supports the business overall.

• When should I consider talking to HR?

I do recommend going to HR as the first line of defense. You should contact HR with one of the three following goals in mind:

1. You might want to obtain a strategic reality check on a dilemma you're having. For example, are you overreacting? Are you in some other way misreading the problem? You will outline the situation you're in, describe what actions you plan to take or have already taken, and ask for an objective but informed, organization-related opinion.
2. You want to obtain support and advice. Here's when you might say: "I think I've gone as far as I can go in my job, I'd really rather be doing something else, and I'd like your help. How do I get out of my department?" In this discussion, you are not attributing your discontent to your boss or other people with whom you work.
3. You want to present a grievance. This is when you report an instance of sexual, racial, age, or other harassment, suspected discrimination, unethical or illegal behavior, or something else of a similarly serious nature. The ombudsman, compliance officer, or legal department might be another venue for presenting your grievance.

It's important to approach HR with a specific and rational mission in mind.

Be clear about your objective. Is it a reality check or advice, or are you there to register a grievance?

continued

• How do I initiate a meeting?

Certainly, it's completely appropriate and a good move to find out who your HR people are and if others in the organization have had occasion to discuss issues with them. Ask your colleagues ("I'm wondering what HR is like here. Have you contacted them for any reason? What has been your experience?").

Call and say you'd like to set up an appointment to talk about a matter that's on your mind.

At your meeting, do not vent. Do not sound hysterical (although you can of course describe feelings of anger, unhappiness, fearfulness, helplessness, or whatever they might be). Don't approach the HR professional as if he or she were a therapist. You are going to a member of management of the organization, so keep your focus on problem solving. HR people are often quite good at counseling, but that's not the primary nature of their role.

To maximize the help you can receive from HR, you must be sensitive to their concerns in addition to your own. They're not your union rep.

• Will my conversation be kept confidential?

HR is the employee's advocate, but is still a member of the management team with obligations to the organization. Therefore, even if you're seeking a reality check, advice, or clarification, do not assume confidentiality. Ask what will be kept confidential and what won't be, and reinforce to the HR professional that you want advice or a reality check, and will try to solve the problem yourself. As a general rule, if you reinforce that you are not presenting a grievance and that you want to take care of the issue yourself, chances are your conversation will remain confidential. But, you want to make sure that is the case. If they cannot guarantee you confidentiality even in an advice situation, and you do not want to initiate a grievance, you should think twice about whether or not you want to put the problem in HR's lap.

continued

If you are presenting a grievance, you cannot expect that your discussion will be kept confidential. Here's why: When an employee reports a specific instance of sexual, racial, age, or other harassment, or suspected illegal discrimination, or some such actionable offense, HR must investigate and intervene wherever required in the chain of command.

However, the difference between getting advice and presenting a grievance is often a very thin line. For example, suppose your boss is trying to seduce you, but you don't want to cause him difficulties by going public. You might arrange an appointment with HR and say, "I'm working with someone who has been making unwanted sexual advances. I do want to keep this matter confidential. I don't want to get this person in trouble, and I'd just like your suggestions. I really would like to know from a reality perspective, what options do I have to say 'no' nicely? What do you think I can do?"

You can probably get confidentiality with such a request. Listen to what HR advises; perhaps discuss the possibility of a transfer.

On the other hand, if the situation has become intolerable, you simply want it to stop, and you believe the boss's behavior should be exposed, you will be presenting a grievance that HR is obligated to act on. It cannot be kept confidential under those conditions.

In all cases, be extremely discreet, diplomatic, and professional in the language you use to describe the circumstances you are reporting, bearing in mind that your complaint might be communicated to others. Any highly wrought or slanderous remarks can rebound on you. HR might need to report what you say to company lawyers. Find a way to communicate the necessary information without hurting yourself.

In addition to being careful about the words you use, however, you can appropriately ask candid questions about next steps and how they might impact you: "If this is reported, will my name be used? What might be the ramifications to my career?"

continued

In my experience, HR professionals are highly ethical. But because they do have to balance the needs of management with the needs of employees, when you're making a grievance that implies management has done something wrong, you can't expect HR to be completely on your side. You might need to obtain your own legal counsel to adequately protect your rights.

- **Even if you do not trust your HR department, go anyway if you have a grievance.**

     Perhaps you have solid reasons not to trust HR. I would still advise arranging for a talk when you have a grievance. In such a case, it's important to go on record with the HR department. They will typically bring in internal and/or external legal resources to initiate an investigation. In this investigation, you might ask for discretion if at all possible regarding the use of your name.

Emily: what happened to her one day on the job

Emily, in her early 40s, the divorced single parent of an 8-year-old, was attending a sales meeting of the Fortune 500 Company for which she worked. A VP, she was director of marketing for one company brand; her boss, John, was head of the marketing division. Because she lived outside the city, Emily had taken a room in the hotel where the meeting was being held, in order to avoid a late commute home. Her boss had mentioned to her that morning that he'd also be staying over in the hotel, somewhat to her surprise—Emily knew he actually lived nearby. When the last session ended, John insisted they have dinner together at a quiet restaurant. Though exhausted, she felt she couldn't say no.

     It was an uncomfortable meal. John rested his hand on her knee several times, began talking about difficulties between him and his wife, and seemed to resist bringing the evening to a close. Finally, Emily got back to her room, sensing she'd narrowly escaped a bad scene.

Emily was beginning to connect the dots. Over the past couple of months, she'd felt anxious in her boss's presence, without quite understanding why. Sometimes she believed John was flirtatious. He often called her in for a talk about business right at the end of the day, when the office had mostly emptied out. He had twice phoned her at home in the evenings to discuss some matter or other, usually catching her just as she was getting her son to bed. In addition, John had recently given her an unexpected and large bonus, one she felt was more than she warranted. Emily had a vague sense of being set up as beholden to her boss.

She wanted to clear the air, yet she was torn. What actually *was* going on? John hadn't actually propositioned her. And she admired him.

One thing she *was* quite sure of was her own part in the scenario playing out so uncomfortably. Her feelings for John remained those of employee to boss and mentor, and she hadn't encouraged him to suspect anything beyond that. (In fact, Emily's steadfastness points to why the boss's behavior can be considered irrational. Had she begun dressing provocatively, suggesting out-of-the-office socializing, and in other ways inviting personal attention—and the boss was responding—John's newly seductive behavior potentially fit the situation. It might not have been politically correct, it might not have befitted his role, but neither was it entirely unreasonable.)

How could Emily handle her tricky job situation—be certain in her own mind what was happening and then, perhaps, approach her boss?

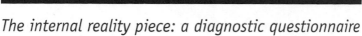
The internal reality piece: a diagnostic questionnaire

Bosses are authority figures in our lives. How we feel about and respond to their behaviors tends to echo patterns relating to those earliest authority figures—parents. In Carl's story above, we looked at some typical responses to a boss who displays anger or disappointment: fury, a wish to hide, rebelliousness, puzzlement. In Emily's story, the internal reality questions are a little different:

• Am I especially eager to please an authority figure?

And was your parent/authority figure relatively benevolent or relatively frightening?

Emily described her father as "dynamic, charismatic." A powerful, dominant man, she always wanted to make him proud of her. At the same time, there was nothing scary or intimidating about him. Her father was kind, very much on her side, a strong mentor who believed in her.

So Emily was programmed to think only the best of dominant, powerful men who were nice to her. She brought to the disconcerting situation at work a largely benign internal reality. Although aware of her discomfort and vague anxiety in the presence of her boss, Emily, in a sense, didn't feel sufficiently paranoid to set limits with him. And that might mean real trouble. If she continued to avoid taking an action, she might essentially enable his irrational behavior by encouraging him to believe she was interested in a personal relationship. What could happen next: Emily finds herself smack in a moment at which she must reject his obvious advances. Then, in all likelihood, her boss would become shamed or enraged, because of her failure to put the brakes on earlier by sending him a warning message.

We could present another face to this story:

- **Am I especially inclined to be suspicious of an authority figure?**

    If Emily's father had been sexually provocative, perhaps almost sexually abusive, her distrust and wariness of male authority figures might provoke in her an overreaction to the boss's behavior. Furious at the inappropriateness of it, she responds prematurely and sets limits too early and too aggressively, long before she's explored the external reality.

    In either scenario, this young woman could shoot herself in the foot, with potentially disastrous consequences.

The external reality piece: a diagnostic questionnaire

- **What kind of boss am I working for?**

    To determine if seductive behavior is coming from the good guy, the politician, or the destructive guy, Emily needs to gather data by following the diagnostic questionnaire I've described above for Carl as he figured out how to approach his difficult boss. For example:

    Being careful not to sound gossipy, not to talk in a way that might hurt her boss, and never to characterize him as a seducer, Emily can try to learn if her boss has engaged in similar behavior with other women. She might ask a female colleague or two if John sometimes suggests they work late. Have they ever been out for drinks with John? Phone calls at home? She might casually say to a coworker, "Tell me a little about John. What's your perception of him as a boss and mentor?"

    Emily would be wise also to watch for further signs that fill out the picture. How is John managing *his* boss these days? Are other male executives seemingly over-friendly with their female subordinates? Are there rumors of corporate changes that might be causing John to feel insecure?

If Emily concludes she's dealing with an overstressed good guy or a politician, there's a strong possibility that he can be persuaded to modify his behavior, once she carefully initiates a talk aimed at setting limits and reestablishing workplace boundaries that have been fading away. If he's a destructive narcissist, her chance of success is less likely.

In the steps that follow, we look at those three possibilities, with approaches that offer her the best chance of soothing her boss, stopping the unwanted behaviors, *and* protecting herself.

- **How have I benefited from my boss's attention, and what do my coworkers think about that?**

Here is a critical piece of the external reality that has nothing to do with the personality of the boss, or whether Emily assesses him as a good guy, a politician, or a destructive guy. Emily received a large bonus. She would be wise to err on the side of caution, and assume that her colleagues know about the windfall and have also observed the boss's personal interest in Emily. And then she would definitely be wise—even if she is able to politely and diplomatically put a brake on the good guy's or the politician's unwanted advances—to arrange a confidential meeting with her HR department and explain the circumstances of her situation. Here's why:

In at least one state, a new law allows employees to sue an organization if they perceive that one employee has received preferential treatment from a boss due to a sexual liaison. Even when nothing's happened between the boss and the employee, the mere perception of preferential treatment—a large bonus, an unexpected promotion, highly desirable assignments—because of a sexual relationship can raise legal concerns and put the organization at risk for litigation. That's something that Emily should want to head off at the pass by taking preventive steps

Best next steps: dealing with the overstressed good guy

Emily decides her boss is a good guy under stress.

She's been working for him for almost two years. She's aware he's just past his 60th birthday; there have been small indications, in addition to the talk over dinner, of marital problems. There might be issues of depression, fear of impotence, or concerns about his career winding down. John has seemed emotionally needy of late. Perhaps, in an effort to feel better, he's turned to this woman with whom he's previously enjoyed a trustworthy relationship. In a vulnerable state, he misunderstands or distorts the respect with which she obviously regards him.

Some pointers for dealing with the seductive boss who's basically a good guy:

• Initiate a talk *before* he has made a clear proposition.

Any woman faced with seductive behavior must make her position clear as soon as she's certain she has read her boss's intentions accurately. You do not want to wait until the proposition, and then say, "I won't have sex with you! How could you suggest such a thing?" Find a moment when the boss is alone and seemingly not preoccupied with an immediate work problem; say you'd appreciate a few minutes of his time in order to discuss an issue that has been on your mind.

• Avoid any creation of seeming intimacy.

Talk to the boss privately—but in the office during work hours, or in a public place, over lunch (not dinner, not at drinks after work). Do not let there be any possibility of misunderstanding or of your feeding perceptions that enable the boss to believe you're agreeable to his overtures.

- ### Maintain a supportive tone and attitude.

    Don't attack in any way. Don't shame him into feeling person-ally rejected. Be conciliatory.

- ### Affirm the positive working relationship you've enjoyed.

    Here's one way Emily might initiate her talk:

    "I have been extremely happy with our relationship as boss and subordinate. Over the past month or two, I've been a little puzzled by some of your comments and actions. They've made me feel as if you might see our relationship in more personal terms than formerly. It's very important you understand that's been unexpected and not some-thing I want to reinforce. What I do want to reinforce is how much I enjoy working for you, and I consider you my boss and my mentor. So I hope we're on the same page."

    If the boss suggests they continue to work over drinks:

    "I really appreciate your attention, John. I feel honored by the time you spend with me, given how busy you are. But I'm having a time management problem of my own. As you know, my son needs my attention in the evening. Often, when you suggest we go out for drinks, I think our work is done for the day. So what I'm asking is, can we reschedule this meeting for the morning, so that I can get home and relieve my babysitter?"

    The overstressed good guy, given the opportunity to retreat gracefully, is likely to respond well to this approach.

Best next steps: dealing with the politician

Emily decides her boss is a politician, the constructive narcissist.

He doesn't seem to be under stress; at least Emily hasn't been able to come up with specific signs. And he's not a bad guy. However, some seismic changes have taken place in the management ranks of the corporation recently, and everybody Emily's talked to is aware of a shift in the workplace atmosphere. A new top boss has come to town, and the man is a macho type, an obvious womanizer. Emily's boss might be imitating that behavior in an effort to ingratiate himself with the new regime.

The strategies mentioned above for the good guy are useful also with this boss. But some additional points to keep in mind:

• Manage his ego carefully.

Generally speaking, once you say to the politically motivated boss, "As much as I admire you, I would like to make sure you understand . . ." and so on, he'll stop the seductive overtures. If he believes his behavior will hurt him professionally, he'll be able to control it. He might find other ways to ape the macho culture, but he won't bother you.

An ego managing statement might sound like this:

"I want to be successful at my job because I want to support you in every way. You've got a hard job, and I'm here to help you. I know myself well enough to know that I'm most motivated under certain conditions and with certain boundaries between us that make me feel comfortable. Not having that, as I've experienced lately, makes it more difficult for me to focus on my work and maintain my objectivity. I'd really appreciate your help here. I'd like you to understand that the best working relationship for me would be the way we worked together formerly."

• Appeal to the boss's sense of success and power.

Emily might start this conversation:

"I know you want me to be as effective as I can be. Of course, you have the prerogative to manage me whichever way you want; you're the boss. But I must tell you that from a quality of work perspective, I really liked our old relationship better. Do you mind very much if we don't have drinks after work? Because frankly, that's taking away from my work and causing me not to be as productive, and I know you don't want that. We've got our job to do here, you and me."

- **Offer further clarification of your meaning only if he asks for it.**

Once you have launched the conversation along these lines, be prepared to hear: "What do you mean? I really have no idea what you're talking about." In that case, it's necessary to go into more detail. If Emily's politician boss responded to her initial statements in this way, she might elaborate:

"Well, John, you know you never used to call me at home and also we never went out for drinks. I think in the past you respected my need to compartmentalize my life. In the last month or two, I've picked up that that's something you're not doing much anymore. You're my boss, you can do what you want, but I would like to go back to the working pattern we enjoyed formerly. It's easier for me to manage my time that way."

If the boss does *not* suggest he's clueless about your meaning, say no more. He got the message.

Best next steps: dealing with the bad guy

Emily decides she's dealing with a destructive narcissist.

She'd only been on the job for four months, the last two of which saw John becoming ever more insistent in his pursuit. After making a few discreet inquiries among coworkers, Emily learned that her boss has a reputation as a philanderer. He might also, someone suggested to her, have an alcohol problem. There were several instances of his seductive behavior with women employees in the past, but he's been able to remain under the radar. One woman who worked for him abruptly quit; another seemed to go along with his inappropriate behavior, perhaps for political purposes. What was especially disturbing to Emily was that her boss could be vindictive and dangerous. He had one woman fired; the consensus was that she'd rebuffed him.

Emily hadn't recognized any of this during her job interview with the boss. He behaved well then, and she had every expectation he'd be a supportive mentor. Now, she was seeing him as a known predator.

Sometimes seductive behavior has a pathological aspect. This man might be a misogynist; possibly he's contemptuous of successful women in his arena and he responds by sexualizing them.

The harsh truth is, at the end of the day Emily has few options open to her. With the destructive boss, there's probably never a strong possibility of successful negotiation. She'll be punished one way or another. The actions she *can* take:

• **Approach a trusted confidant.**

Due to the complexity of the situation, before taking any internal or external action, perhaps you will want to discuss the specifics with an ethical, reliable individual within the company who can give suggestions on how to hadle matters.

• **Search out the appropriate vehicle within the organization that deals with these concerns.**

Emily's predicament involved seductive behavior from the boss. Seductive behavior is not sexual harassment. It becomes harassment if the unwanted advances don't stop, despite all efforts. Most organizations tend to be enormously sensitive to seductive behavior from management because of their concerns over claims of sexual harassment. When there is sexual harassment, it's appropriate to present a grievance.

- **Protect yourself.**

   If yours is a severe situation that reflects sexual harassment and you are not getting the response from the organization that you would expect, consider talking with an employment attorney for advice (see the side bar on page 44 for further information on approaching an employment attorney). Start keeping a record of the boss's behavior as well as your own. Be prepared for the possibility that the boss may be setting you up to be fired if you reject him.

   Emily's best move might be looking for a new job, soon.

- **Go on record with HR**

   This step applies to all three possible scenarios.

   Even if you have successfully diffused an uncomfortable but basically benign situation with a good guy or a politician boss, you still must be aware of the possible perception by colleagues that you've received preferential treatment because of a sexual liaison. At a confidential meeting with HR, clarify the reality of your situation. Emily, for example, should put herself on record that no sexual relationship exists or existed between herself and her boss, though some behaviors may have been perceived by others to indicate one. She states that she requests confidentiality, she is solving the issue herself, and she simply wants to provide HR with the facts. In so doing, she covers herself and protects the organization.

Some more difficult bosses

At the beginning of this chapter on the difficult boss, I mentioned that the breed comes in various shapes and forms. We might also single out:

- **The dependent boss**

   Insecure, fearful, worrying about keeping his job, he relies heavily on you, his talented employee—to such a degree that he

LAWYERS

• When should I consider seeking legal advice?

Internal support services in the form of an HR function, an employee assistance program, or a legal counsel department might not exist in your company. Smaller organizations might have a designated person for matters of compensation and benefits, but not for employee relations. Perhaps as far as you have determined, there's no one in the organization to talk to if you are convinced you're being set up by a boss who's out to fire you, for example. Or perhaps your attempts to work out your problem haven't been successful or fruitful with the in-house professionals.

Legal advice—going to an attorney outside the organization—is a wise survival strategy when internal resources are not available or responsive. If you're embroiled in a trigger situation concerning a boss, a subordinate, or a peer, and you feel there's a real possibility your reactions to it might backfire and you might indeed face termination or a liability situation, get help. When you are beginning to sense the outcome to your situation won't be good, or you need political advice, speaking to an employment lawyer outside the firm about options to protect yourself is a good proactive move.

In particular, if you plan to protest an action taken against you and openly confront the situation in a corporate environment, you really need to talk to an attorney. You will potentially set up a problem that will require you to leave. In that case, an attorney can be helpful in working out a severance package and other particulars.

• How should I prepare myself to see a lawyer?

It's critically important to keep a detailed diary of the situation and the behavior that's occurring, before you ever contact an attorney. Write down dates on which, for example, you initiated

continued

what you hoped to be a problem-solving discussion with the boss, peer, or subordinate. Write down the nature of the conversation, what points of view were shared, what was promised, what follow-up actions were agreed upon, and so on. Keep this diary in a confidential file outside of work, and certainly not on the organization's computer.

Should you ever find yourself in a defensive position—you are accused of harassment or discrimination by a subordinate, for example, after you have taken corrective action—you won't have to rely on your memory alone. You will have a chronological history.

• How can I locate a good employment lawyer?

In a confidential manner, ask friends, family, or trusted colleagues for suggestions. If you wish to be discreet, say you're helping someone else who's looking for a good employment lawyer. You might receive referrals from various sources. For example, a friend who works in another organization with an employee assistance program might obtain useful referral information for you.

If you come up empty handed through those channels, research the local Chamber of Commerce for legal aid resources. Contact the bar association in your state for referrals as well.

• Should I retain the lawyer I locate?

My advice: Don't. Initially, offer to pay her hourly rate for occasional advice. In my experience, when an attorney is on retainer, there is an expectation that an action will be taken involving some form of separation from the company and now it's time to negotiate. In many cases, that's probably not your goal.

You don't want to retain an overly aggressive attorney whose demeanor might suggest litigation. This individual might prematurely

continued

> push the buttons of the organization, and your worst fears will be fulfilled—you present yourself as a victim, you fight the company, they want you out, and you're gone.
>
> Unless you have already decided you will litigate and you ask an attorney to prepare a complaint or perhaps negotiate your separation from the company, talk to the lawyer purely for information gathering or strategy building. Use her as an advisor, pay by the hour, and go to her as the need arises.

resists encouraging you to move on to bigger and better things. The development of subordinates is part of the supervisor's role. But the dependent boss wants you to remain right where you are, taking care of him and making him look good.

If you happened to be the adult child of dependent, dysfunctional parents, you might be used to this kind of behavior and comfortable with it; that's a blind spot that can cause you to stay put, not challenge the boss, and risk limiting your career opportunities. On the other hand, if you wanted to get far away from the old parent/child pattern, you might find your dependent boss infuriating. You'll have to be careful about overreacting, being insubordinate, or in other ways mismanaging your situation.

• The impulsive boss

He's reactive, emotional, not equipped from experience to supervise people or manage resources. He's not a hostile individual, but he yells a lot. In his offices there are frequent scenes, last-minute changes of direction, sudden emergencies, little planning. The impulsive boss tends to be found most often in a creative environment, where such behavior might be culturally acceptable.

Does your background include parents who were erratic and

volatile, but also high functioning and good to you? You might have a great deal of tolerance for the impulsive boss; his behavior doesn't bother you. There's a blind spot that works. On the other hand, if your parents' style caused you real pain, you'll need to control a tendency to react to your new authority figure either too aggressively or by withdrawing.

• The panicky boss

This difficult boss always anticipates the worst. She creates doomsday scenarios (*we're all going to lose our jobs!*), keeping you in a state of anxiety. Because she's panicky, she constantly asks you to work longer hours, double-check things that don't need to be checked, meet deadlines earlier than is necessary.

External reality is the key to understanding and reacting to the panicky boss. If her behavior seems appropriate, because of organizational or economic changes, you'll want to protect yourself from being used, without challenging her. If she's a good guy going through bad personal times, she needs your reassurance. However, if she's new to the job and clearly in over her head, you have a decision to make—continue working for her or leave?

• The micromanager/overcontroller

This boss has to have his finger in everything. Maybe his behaviors are reasonable for the moment, because of an emergency situation or because the strategic demands of the business require his technical expertise.

But the micromanager will be especially hard to live with if you have an entrepreneurial spirit and you took the job with the understanding that he'd be a hands-off boss. One blind spot you'll need to beware of: When you're controlled or overly managed, you feel trapped, and then betrayed. Your inclination is to get out of there fast—without trying to negotiate a better understanding with the boss.

The process I have outlined in this chapter applies to all scenarios: Understand and cope with your internal reality—in particular, try to recognize what feelings are triggered by your own experiences growing up with the parents you had. Gather information about the external reality, in order to come up with an accurate assessment of the environment. Then, figure out the most refined strategic response, so that you come out of a troublesome predicament whole.

3

SUPERCOMPETITIVE PEERS

HOW TO COPE WITH A POTENTIAL FOE
(AND FORGET ABOUT SIBLING RIVALRY)

If you grew up with a brother or sister or two, chances are you experienced your fair share of sibling rivalry. That might have taken the form of which one of you Mom or Dad (you thought) liked best, or arguments over possessions or space. Maybe you remember sharing a scrappy childhood, with lots of (mostly) good-natured tussling. Maybe the two or more of you were engaged in ferocious one-upping when it came to school grades or athletic achievements.

Now, as an adult, echoes of those old competitive urges and rivalries can easily sound in the office. The coworker who's closest to a sibling in relationship terms is going to be the one on a par with you as to rank and degree of power. That's a coworker with whom you might find yourself hitting heads.

With so many companies today thinning out staff to cut costs or accommodate mergers, more people are vying for the same slots.

Competition is on the upswing, with perfectly normal feelings of jealousy being triggered. And there's nothing necessarily wrong with that. Often, jostling for position can spark healthy and productive competition among peers. If you're sharing a title and job description with two coworkers in your office, all of you after the same thing, aren't you likely to step on the gas and work more determinedly to achieve recognition, promotions, or perks?

"Good" competition, of course, is very much aided when a company clearly values teamwork and cooperation. On the other hand, organizations that pit employees against one another in a test of survival, where shark behavior is rewarded, tend to increase unhealthy displays of competitiveness, regardless of what's going on inside the individuals themselves.

In this chapter, we look at the dark side, and how the bad behaviors of a competitive peer can trigger responses that don't serve you well and that even might be self-defeating. A peer's unpleasant, negative actions can take the form of assuming credit for work you've done, pushing you out of the spotlight, withholding important information, belittling your performance publicly or behind your back, making snide remarks, spreading rumors about your personal life or supposed failures, and in the worst-case scenarios, outright acts of sabotage or fraud. This negative competitor typically comes in one of two types. Here, we look at:

- The unintentional backstabber—and how employee Phil coped
- The intentional, bullying backstabber—and how employee Megan coped

Distinguishing between the two isn't always so easy. Once you've figured out just what kind of supercompetitive peer you're dealing with, and once you have brought your own sibling rivalry responses under control, you're in a good position to neutralize a potentially damaging situation.

Phil's story: what happened to him one day on the job

Phil and Brian shared space in an open bullpen type office. Both in their early 30s, they were associates at a large corporation in the financial services industry. Each was trying to establish a solid reputation within the company, building up a client list and researching investment opportunities. Each had their sights set on a vice presidency.

The men had enjoyed an amiable relationship for a couple of years, until Brian started acting in ways that annoyed Phil. On three occasions when Phil had stepped out of the area for a brief time he returned to find Brian at his desk and talking on his phone. The conversations were animated and clearly business related, and in each case it turned out that Brian had been taking a call from one of Phil's clients. Brian did pass along the message that so-and-so had called. When Phil returned the calls sometime later, he learned that Brian had questioned these individuals about their financial goals and suggested various new avenues of investment. The clients—Phil's people—were impressed and wanted to know more. To Phil, it seemed that his officemate was horning in on his territory, maybe even trying to steal away customers.

Cold calling—when an associate arranged a visit with a potential new investor—was highly valued by the company brass. This was generally regarded as the sign of an ambitious employee who was good at scouting out fresh business for the firm. Each associate was expected to give an end-of-month accounting of his activities in this regard. Brian had begun asking Phil about his cold calls—how many he'd racked up, how many were looking promising. When Phil shared this information with him, he later found out that Brian always topped him by one or two contacts. "He really seemed to be going out of his way to show me up," Phil said. "I know for a fact that when he got my numbers, and they were better than his, he'd hustle around for a few days and get in touch with some long lost cousins or something and tout them as new clients."

There was more: At group meetings, when Phil made an observation or a minireport on an investment option he was exploring, Brian always had something to say right afterwards, picking up the thread as if he too was on top of that picture. "The way he'd pop in," Phil said, "he made it sound like he was also looking into this area. Or the two of us were on it together, so actually it didn't come across to the others like I'd come up with the idea myself—which I did. This guy was always jumping on my bandwagon."

All of this was infuriating Phil. He became convinced that Brian was out to trash his career, make him look bad. His initial reaction was one of total distrust, and a strong feeling that he had to battle it out or quit, because the situation was that serious. Phil moved into survival mode, feeling his job was in jeopardy.

Negative competitiveness from a peer should not be allowed to continue. In those situations, perpetually looking the other way or turning the other cheek is almost always a mistake. Before taking action, analyze your feelings and emotional responses, manage those that are likely only to make the picture worse, and try to understand the roots of your coworker's behaviors. Phil, for one, was flying off the handle. He needed to figure out why that was by exploring his internal reality.

The internal reality piece: a diagnostic questionnaire

Consider:

- **How am I feeling about how my supercompetitive peer is acting?**

    Is your instinct to kill the guy? Do the same thing to him that he's doing to you, only worse?

    Or, are you not entirely happy about what's going on, but tell yourself it's no big deal?

Or, are you baffled? You think something's not quite right, but it's probably all in your imagination? Maybe you're in the wrong somehow?

Do you want to report right to your boss and have him take care of the problem?

While you're putting a finger on just what you are feeling, remember that what happened long ago in your family of origin—and perhaps is still going on today, to one degree or another—is very likely triggering your responses in the office. So ask yourself:

- **What was sibling rivalry like back at home, when we were kids?**

Phil's reaction—the intensity of his outrage toward Brian and his survival mode, battle it out attitude—could be traced to his childhood experiences. He'd grown up with one brother, the two boys a year apart in age, and he believed that his father loved and favored his brother over him. "My dad thought Mike hung the moon and I was just sort of there," Phil said. "And this isn't just my fantasy. Mike got the treats, I got what was left over." Phil had kept score, and he gave examples— Mike was bought the electric guitar and amps, Mike got to go to a fancy private college. "When my dad looked at Mike, he always sort of beamed. When he looked at me, he always sort of frowned."

Sibling rivalry was fierce, and Phil grew up with real antipathy towards his brother. He felt shortchanged, as if he had been handed a raw deal. Even now as an accomplished adult, Phil harbored deep-seated feelings that the environment would never make things even or fair, he had to fight for everything he got.

He reflected on all this and he began to consider that he might be overreacting to his coworker Brian. He also started to manage his emotions better by, for one thing, telling himself that his job was probably not at risk in any real way.

Think about your sibling issues.

At the opposite extreme from ferocious rivalry is a family dynamic in which everyone gets along so cooperatively that negative competition from a coworker on the job now is hardly recognizable as such—siblings/peers just aren't expected to act that way.

And then there's the dynamic in which turning to mom or dad was par for the course, a way to score points or bring down punishment on a sibling who was being mean.

An internal reality analysis should, at the least, help to remind you that your coworker is not your brother or sister and the office isn't home. You can, and perhaps should, do things differently than you did in that other environment.

• Have I provoked my peer's behaviors in some way?

Have you unwittingly or unintentionally goaded this person into a competition on the job?

Do recognize in yourself a tendency to flaunt or brag about your accomplishments, perhaps causing the other person to feel on shakier ground even if that's not your intention?

Have you been less than helpful, when a little help was called for?

Could you be a nicer, kinder individual?

Any personal interaction between people who work closely together is always a *pas de deux*, of course, with both sides contributing to the atmosphere. Especially if you conclude you've been a little over the top in your actions, making adjustments in your own behaviors might improve theirs.

Once you have a handle on your side of the problem, investigate the other side as objectively as you can.

The external reality piece: a diagnostic questionnaire

One aim now is to determine whether your coworker is guilty of an intentional or an unintentional act of negative competition.

If it's intentional, this person is out to make you look bad.

If it's unintentional, this person is out to make himself look better.

That's a crucial difference in how you will go about putting a stop to negative competitiveness, and it can be uncovered through some due diligence on your part. What does the external reality in your workplace reveal? So think:

- ## How bad, really, is the behavior of my supercompetitive peer?

  Stealing your work and passing it off as his/her own is pretty bad. So is spreading falsehoods or denigrating your performance to others. Many unpleasant kinds of behaviors, however, fall into a grayer area. Yes, they're out of line and yes, you plan to see that they don't continue—but how evil are they?

  Perhaps the best way to reach an accurate analysis is to ask: Are this person's actions interfering with my doing my work, threatening my job, damaging my reputation, and/or ensuring that I'll never get ahead in this company? If the answer is no, maybe the ramifications aren't as bad as you thought.

  Phil decided that though Brian was taking more credit than he should, jumping on the Phil bandwagon, he never actually tried to put Phil down or suggest he was messing up on the job. And although Brian's behaviors seemed focused on trying to make himself look smarter, a go-getter, and maybe showing off a little at Phil's expense, it wasn't more destructive than that.

- ## What's my track record with this coworker?

  If it's generally and overall been benign—the two of you have worked together for a while, you've known him to be a decent guy—you're probably right to assume no truly malevolent motives behind his currently bothersome actions.

- **What seems to be going on with this person? Where is this behavior coming from?**

Life, as we all know, sometimes gangs up on us. Family demands, money worries, any one of a number of realities can increase stress that becomes displayed in negative ways in the workplace. The supercompetitive peer without evil motives might be under such pressures and feel particularly insecure. Perhaps he's fearful of losing his job, and overcompensating by trying to get as much attention for himself as possible. In the process, he's blocking the view of his coworker. But the comments he makes or his actions are not fiercely devaluing anyone; he's simply overinflating himself.

Try to gauge that situation.

If your coworker has shifted from a cooperative peer into a negatively competitive one, there might be extenuating circumstances that might be pressuring him at the moment.

Phil pursued this line of investigation. "I made a point of observing Brian, and it struck me that he seemed more nervous, jumpy, than he used to be. We never talked about personal stuff for some reason, but we used to crack jokes a lot. I realized that had sort of stopped. He looked distracted sometimes." Phil ran into a coworker in another department, a man he knew was Brian's friend, and mentioned casually that Brian seemed preoccupied lately. "This guy told me that he asked Brian the other day how's it going, and Brian said, 'Well, in the last five months my wife got pregnant, I saw a cardiologist, and I took out a second mortgage. How do you think it's going?' " Phil had some information that probably helped explain his peer's recent behaviors.

On the other hand: let's assume you have little history with this person, you haven't worked together long enough to know much about him as a human being, and your careful explorations suggest no unusual crises or stresses in his life. Maybe he's just flat-out insecure and uncertain. Or maybe in *his* family of origin going one better than the other siblings was normal, just part of the game. In either scenario, you want to analyze if he's truly out to do you harm. If he's not, you will probably have an easier time of reining in his negative competitiveness.

• What's the corporate culture?

Are you working for an organization that rewards shark behavior?

You've observed that the Machiavellian types have the bosses' ears, get the promotions, and leave bodies in their wake on the way up?

If so, realize that you might not be able to rely on appropriate corporate support if you decide you must take your complaints about a supercompetitive peer up the chain of command. In which case you might have difficult decisions to weigh about whether or not you should be there in the first place, an issue that will be examined later in the book.

But a generally benign, team-oriented environment might also be going through a period of downsizing and consolidation. Everyone is aware that fewer positions will be opening up. Consequently, there are environmental causes for real concern. For example, it might have become apparent that Phil or Brian, but not both, would eventually be promoted to a vice president's spot. So Brian, the more insecure of the two, might be responding to this added pressure in the ways he's demonstrated—exaggerating his contribution, bragging a little, trying to shift recognition away from his peer. This is a piece of the external reality that Phil can file away for consideration on how he plans to address Brian. Certainly, it can help diminish his inclination to lash out. Brian's behavior is a little more understandable.

Phil concluded from all of this that Brian was a pressured fellow desperate to get ahead. None of Brian's efforts to take center stage seemed to involve destroying Phil in the process. But Phil still needed to reverse the negative competitiveness.

Best next steps

• Ignore specific behaviors, for a while anyway.

This is a realistic option. In the simplest situation—the negative behaviors are relatively slight and not seriously threatening to your position—you might decide to say nothing for the moment. At the same time:

• Act friendlier.

Or, as the saying goes, keep your friends close and your enemies closer.

If you've determined you are dealing with a formerly cooperative peer who's undergoing internal or external pressures, you might just try to defuse the competitiveness and win over your coworker by treating him with extra kindness. Be supportive. Make him feel a little more important and valued, and underscore the point that you're both on the same team.

So Phil might see an opportunity to throw an investment tip Brian's way, something he's not planning to follow up on himself. He might suggest they go out to lunch or stop for a beer after work. Without sounding like a total phony, he lets Brian know that he likes him as a person and it's enjoyable to spend time together.

This might or might not work. It's worked if after a brief spell of increased friendliness on your part, the guy acts friendly back and the bad behaviors begin diminishing or vanish. On the other hand, if matters don't improve, it's time to move up a notch.

• Have a chat with your competitive peer.

In a pleasant tone, say:

"Look, we like each other; we've had a good relationship. I've noted that in the last few months things have changed a little. For example, in the meeting we just had, I think you presented the distribution of our work not as fairly as I would have expected. I know that you don't mean to compete with me in an unfair way, and I'd expect that's not going to happen again."

Do not say: "You're way out of line, buddy, you don't respect me, I'm going to the boss." Your conversation must be nowhere near as aggressive as that; avoid any language that might intensify the problem. The attempt is to defuse and disarm the competitor, and simply let him know that you have recognized patterns you don't like.

Any such chat, by the way, should be face-to-face or over the phone. Never use e-mail as the vehicle for communicating critical news. If you want to send an e-mail saying, "I'm glad we had that talk this morning, I hope things will improve," that's probably safe. But no more than that.

• Keep notes.

Any time you initiate a conversation in which you're basically challenging another person about his behavior and requesting that he cease and desist, document that talk. Make notes for yourself. At some future point, you might need to refresh your memory about exactly when and how you made a good faith effort to improve matters.

Phil got a grip on his own going-into-battle instincts, behaved in a friendlier and supportive manner towards his supercompetitive peer, and was pleased to see that Brian changed for the better. What if he hadn't?

Suppose you have taken the above steps, and not only have matters not improved but your coworker is behaving even more egregiously? Maybe now you need to escalate the encounter to another level. Maybe, in fact, you were mistaken in your initial assessment, and you're dealing with a genuinely evil backstabber. We explore these possibilities next.

Megan's story: what happened to her one day on the job

Megan, 32, and Shawna, 33, were both account executives with a public relations firm specializing in the promotion of video games and interactive entertainment. They'd worked side by side for about half a year in essentially similar jobs.

These were two bright and talented young women, both MBAs and both hard workers. From the start of their association, Megan was not drawn to Shawna. "Not long after I got to know her, I decided she was a duplicitous kind of person," Megan said. "I once overheard her making a really vicious crack about one of the managers, and then I watched her being smarmy with this same manager the next day in a meeting. I guess that's not so unusual, making fake nice with one of the bosses, but it's something I dislike in a person."

She found other personal qualities unattractive as well. "Shawna was cold. If you passed her in the hall, you never knew if she was going to say hello to you or not. But she was fearless in reaching out to the clients. I found her challenging in that way."

Megan had no problem with being challenged. Working near an ambitious, results-oriented person like Shawna tended to energize her. They weren't going to be friends, but she was able to compartmentalize her feelings: Personally, she found Shawna not too likeable; professionally, she found a lot to admire. Then Shawna began behaving in more pointedly unpleasant ways toward her, though Megan initially was in the dark about some of that.

At one of the departmental meetings, Shawna gave a report on the commitments she'd landed during a recent trade show. Their boss asked Megan what she'd come up with. Megan replied she hadn't been aware that she was expected to attend the show. The boss was puzzled. "I wrote both of you a memo about that."

On another occasion, Megan sent the boss a note about feedback she'd received from one of their distributors. The boss stopped by her office the next day. "Shawna came in to talk to me this morning on this same problem," he said. "I think she's come up with a better way to handle it, so I'm going with that."

Small incidents were adding up, but Megan wasn't genuinely alarmed until a coworker suggested they go out for a coffee break. "Listen, Megan," she said, "watch out for Shawna. She's bad news." Shawna had made thinly veiled comments to the coworker and others in their department hinting that Megan had an addiction problem. Referring to the two-week vacation Megan had recently taken, Shawna dropped the term "rehab."

Megan started putting two and two together.

The intentional evil backstabber, who acts as Shawna did towards her coworker, is typically skilled at coercion and takes pride in her ability to inflict damage or wield control. She might deride, sabotage, or put down someone else. Unlike the first category of the supercompetitive peer, this individual isn't primarily trying to demonstrate that her expertise is superior or bragging that she's better. That might be one upshot of her behaviors. She might gain power through those tactics, but behind it all is a real intent to hurt. She's a bully.

These people are more difficult than those in the first category, and clearly the most problematic. So a careful internal and external exploration is in order.

The internal reality piece: a diagnostic questionnaire

- **What were my sibling relationships like?**

Once again, useful clues might be found in remembering how life went on between you and your brothers or sisters.

Was there a great deal of competition, and what was its nature? Mean-spirited? Rough and tumble?

Megan was used to a competitive environment, in fact. She had grown up in a family of four girls, and the sisters were always vying against one another, but it all took place within a solidly supportive and good-natured atmosphere. No doubt in large part thanks to the wise and loving parenting they received, the four girls would push each other relentlessly—and also defend each other to the death and applaud each other's accomplishments. So Megan tended to underreact to Shawna's provocations, and wasn't sufficiently sensitive to the real damage her peer was out to inflict. In a sense, she took it as a kind of tough, competitive play.

She needed to tell herself: This is not the past. I must act to protect myself.

• How have I been responding towards my supercompetitive peer?

Of course, beware of any culpability on your part, any ways you might have antagonized this individual and so unleashed her baser inclinations. But short of being an evil backstabber yourself, chances are you're innocent.

So focus on your reactive behavior:

Have you been ignoring bullying negative competitiveness when it has clearly become a dangerous and damaging pattern?

Are you starting to respond in kind, determined to fight fire with fire? When you're facing an evil backstabbing coworker, that's a fight you won't win and you'll hurt your reputation in the process.

Do you tend to become apologetic, or overly defensive?

Are you ready to tell all to your boss, before you've tried to deal with the matter on your own?

None of that is good. Bring your emotional responses under control, and then conduct your due diligence.

The external reality piece: a diagnostic questionnaire

- ### **What exactly has my supercompetitive peer been up to?**

You need to figure out as best as possible just what this individual has done or is doing.

Can you obtain concrete evidence? This reality effort might take you into the nitty-gritty realm of trying to determine if papers have been removed from your desk or if your computer files have been opened by someone else. It might involve backtracking an incident that now arouses your suspicions. For example, Megan might ask her boss if he retained a copy of the memo he'd sent about the trade show, and if she could see it now—which might confirm in her own mind that she'd never read it, perhaps because it had been intercepted.

Can you ask coworkers if they have been aware of negative comments about you made by the peer?

Have there been more subtle attempts to undermine your confidence?

Megan told this story: "My group had a lot of meetings, and Shawna invariably did something that completely rattled me. I'd make some contribution to the discussion, present an idea, and the talk would move on to someone else. And I'd become aware that Shawna, across the conference table, would continue looking at me. Everyone would have turned attention to the person now talking, but Shawna would be staring at me. So I'd look over at her, maybe smile, and she would just keep this blank stare on me. Of course my inclination was to assume she found what I'd said irrelevant. It took me a while to realize this, but the stare was a clear intimidation tactic."

- ### **What is the climate of this company?**

As I mentioned earlier, some organizations seem to promote and thrive on a dog-eat-dog, let-the-best-man-win atmosphere. That's an atmosphere that might be created and reflected down from the highest levels of the corporation, and it shouldn't be that difficult to recognize once you've tuned your radar to the issue. You're trying to find out if the kind of negative competitive behavior your peer has engaged in is generally applauded or sanctioned. Some questions you might try to answer for yourself:

Has my superior picked up on my coworker's obvious attempts to make me look bad? And if he has, has he given signals that he wants to curb that behavior or, on the other hand, signals that he's kind of relishing the in-fighting?

Do the higher-ups in the company work well together or do they seem to be pitted against each other?

If you conclude that yours is a team culture, there's a good probability that if and when you go to management or HR, you'll find support. That gives you more leverage. On the other hand, when the organizational climate is one that rewards shark behavior, and your coworker's actions are typical, you might not get much satisfaction when you do confront your competitive peer. That's grounds for some further investigation:

- ### What wiggle room do I have here?

Is there a job you can transfer into where you will not have to work with this peer?

Best next steps

- ### Do not react in kind.

This bears repeating. Whenever the negative competitive behavior absolutely must be controlled—when it's a public assault of some kind, when it's not easily excusable—do not attempt to exact tit for tat. Preserve the moral high ground.

- **On occasion, address the bully head on in a nonassaultive manner.**

Suppose you're at a group meeting and your supercompetitive peer makes a snide, sarcastic comment at your expense. There's no reason why you have to ignore it. Ignoring it, giving no response, makes you look weak. So in an assertive way, say: "That remark is out of line. We'll need to discuss this, and let's do that later."

You don't want to start a battle then and there, but you have made it clear you're not letting the matter drop.

- **Attempt to disarm your attacker.**

This is step one of a confrontation, in which you approach your peer in a more intimate setting without attacking or risking escalation of the situation.

Megan waited until Shawna was alone in her office, and said casually: "Shawna, are there problems between us?" Then she listened quietly, nondefensively to what Shawna had to say, which was a denial that any problem existed. Megan replied: "Gee, you know I understand from others [not divulging who the others are] that you've been saying certain things about me that aren't very flattering and that actually aren't true. I'm a little puzzled by that and I'd like to discuss it with you."

Shawna insisted that Megan must have heard wrong, all was fine.

Megan responded: "Well, I'm glad to know that. Just in case, if in the future you have any problems with me, I'd like you to talk to me directly."

Sometimes, just letting your competitive peer know you're on to her helps, even if she's not owning up to what she's been doing. She realizes she has been caught, and she starts acting better.

Or, this individual keeps right on with the negative behaviors.

• Put your peer on notice.

When a coworker's actions are highly negative, and you are convinced this person is systematically out to get you, it's time to force a more direct accounting and outline the next actions you will take. In this talk, do not sound as if you're about to complain that afternoon to your supervisor, but you can certainly suggest that might be a recourse you'll have to take eventually.

Megan, for example, can say something like this:

"We've worked together for a while now, but your behavior lately has really not been respectful. I've had information that you've been saying things behind my back; I mentioned this to you before. I want you to call a halt. If you don't, I expect I will have to go to senior management and report this behavior, because I consider it unethical. I would hope that we could resolve this between the two of us. I'm not your enemy and I expect you not to be mine. There's enough room for both of us. But, if you don't change these tactics, I'm going to have to deal with it."

So you have said—in a nice way—that if the behavior doesn't stop, you will have no choice but to report it to your boss, whom you share in common. If you don't share a boss, then it will be to a senior manager in the organization. You have firmly and politely put her on notice: You asked her once, you have now asked her twice, and if things don't change you will bring the difficult situation to a higher level.

In any of these talks, do not reveal your feelings; doing so will only weaken you. Keeping a lid on in that manner might go against your instincts; after all, when we're dealing with a friend or a healthy subordinate or peer, it probably comes naturally to say something like, "Look, when you do this kind of thing I feel completely frustrated and upset." When you're dealing with a bully, don't give away your feelings in that manner. With this individual, you must appear strong.

• Document your conversations.

Again, keep careful notes for yourself of the steps you have taken in your attempt to resolve the matter. Keep a detailed record of any clear acts of sabotage you uncovered in your reality check.

• Bring the negative competitiveness to management's attention.

If the backstabbing continues, report it. You do not want to come across like a tattletale; therefore it's critical to be armed with those concrete facts and to explain what actions you've already undertaken. You must also stress (in order to avoid the tattletale impression) that your coworker's behavior is upsetting teamwork and not good for the business.

Megan might say something like this:

"These are the facts about what Shawna's been up to. I have discussed this with her. Shawna was defensive and denied any culpability. I still believe she has culpability. I would like some counsel from you about what leverage there exists in the organization, considering that these behaviors are interfering with productivity and teamwork. What's your best advice?" Megan should then make a record of this conversation.

If the department is large or employees work across departments, you might suggest to the boss that making inquiries and providing information to HR would be an appropriate action to take. Possibly others have put in similar complaints about this individual, and that's something the boss should know.

• Decide if you can remain.

It's necessary to gauge the risks you are willing to take and the fortitude you are able to muster. After you intervene with your bullying peer, watch what happens subsequently, document your exchanges, and talk to management, you might realize that the bad behaviors have not changed and the company is essentially not supportive to your concerns. What then?

Megan might then have to make a decision: Can she toughen up and learn to be more of a combatant with her coworker, hone the fine art of being a warrior? She might do that with some support in the form of outside coaching. (Information about coaching appears on page 90.) Or, is this just not the way she wants to live her life? Should she find another environment in which a team culture is valued and bad guys are not tolerated?

At the beginning of this chapter, I mentioned the difficulty of figuring out just whom you're dealing with—the unintentional, probably insecure competitor or the intentional, evil backstabber. Sometimes you won't know if a solution works or not until you put it into practice and then observe what happens after that and over time. Sometimes you won't understand the real source of the problem until you behave with such political correctness that your coworker ultimately shows his colors.

Unless the behavior is blatantly destructive, assume the best-case scenario. Then control emotions that come out of old patterns and that cause you to be maladaptive, and forge ahead in the ways we've outlined here.

4

THE TROUBLED OR TROUBLESOME SUBORDINATE

HOW TO COACH A DIFFICULT ASSISTANT (AND RESIST THE URGE TO PARENT)

In any reasonably sized company, the employees resemble a normal sample of the general population, falling along a bell curve in terms of likeability and productivity. On one end are the few easy-going, high performers, the people who are a joy to work with and cause no big headaches for anyone. On the other end exist the few impossible individuals, the ones who get everyone's stomach acid churning. As in life, the great majority of employees fall somewhere in between.

If you are in a managerial position of any sort and the person or people you're managing are the easy-going, high-performing joys, you no doubt feel extremely fortunate or extremely competent as a leader of others, possibly both. Over the course of a career, however, you can almost surely expect to find yourself sooner or later dealing with a troubled or troublesome subordinate. This individual can come in many shapes and forms, but in this chapter I identify the four most common categories and describe the difficulties each presents to his or her manager. We look at:

- The temporarily stressed subordinate who's still getting the job done—and how manager Mary Ellen coped
- The impaired subordinate whose work is falling off—and how manager Robert coped
- The blaming subordinate who's creating havoc—and how manager Bill coped
- The competent subordinate who lacks people skills—and how manager Vincent coped

Here's the common thread: You, the manager, are in the superior position and hold more power in this than in your other relationships on the job . . . very much like being a real-life parent to a real-life child or children. When it comes to managing difficult subordinates, who might be behaving like clingy toddlers, dreamy preteens, or abrasive adolescents, parenting tendencies can be triggered—and you might be ill prepared for your reactions. Whatever the response, coping with a troubled or troublesome subordinate can exact significant stress.

It's extremely common for managers to slide unwittingly into the role of parent. Depending on temperament, early parenting history, or actual parenting style at the time, responses can range from overprotectiveness and overindulgence, to harsh, punitive, or autocratic acting out. Besides taking on parenting roles, managers often experience feelings that are familiar to many mothers and fathers of minor children—anger, frustration, impotence to control irrational behavior, guilt, responsibility, exhaustion, or just a sense of being very badly used by someone who shouldn't be doing that. In the grip of such emotions, behaviors that are nonproductive and that perhaps even exacerbate the problem at hand are all too likely to emerge.

Many of us haven't been taught how to be great parents. Neither have we been taught how to be great managers. But develop the philosophy that learning to identify, cope, and deal with a difficult subordinate is a skill; that it takes time and experience to master; that mistakes are not irreversible; and that outside advice is often crucial, and the job becomes easier.

The following scenarios describe my four categories of the troubled or troublesome subordinate. As you will see, in each one the basic goals are the same: first, manage your own reactions; second, take careful note of the employee's difficult behaviors; and third, effectively intervene to change or control those behaviors in order to maximize his or her effectiveness in an ethical and humane way within corporate guidelines. In some situations, as you will also see, it might become necessary to process that individual out of the organization entirely.

Manager Mary Ellen's story: what happened to her one day on the job

Mary Ellen, 45, was the office manager for a postproduction film editing studio, in charge of commercial scheduling and the many day-to-day operations of a fast-paced office. Working as her administrative assistant was 24-year-old Chrissy, a bright young woman who'd been on the job for about a year when difficulties began cropping up.

Chrissy's job involved a lot of paperwork and a fair amount of phone time, confirming appointments with clients, relaying information from the editors, and working with outside suppliers. She was doing that job well. But Chrissy also looked teary-eyed a lot of the time, and was occasionally overheard in a long, agitated phone conversation that wasn't related to film editing. One early evening before everyone headed home, Mary Ellen asked her assistant casually if all was okay. Chrissy piled into Mary Ellen's office, sat down, and poured out a sad story: she'd broken up with her boyfriend, her roommate had moved out of town, she wasn't having any luck finding another compatible roommate, she was terrified about handling the apartment expenses on her own, and worst of all, her mother had recently been diagnosed with cancer.

Mary Ellen felt terrible for her assistant, whom she liked and valued, and immediately suggested that Chrissy might be able to have additional leave time. A few days off seemed to ease the young woman's worries, but her emotional and practical troubles clearly continued. Over the next three months, she increasingly turned to her boss, coming to expect the after-work talk sessions on a daily basis. Mary Ellen took Chrissy out to lunch on several occasions, let her vent, and tried to be comforting.

Then the company acquired several huge new contracts, and Mary Ellen's job demands practically doubled overnight. When Chrissy wanted to talk, Mary Ellen now felt irritated with her—and then guilty about feeling irritated. "I didn't have the time for this anymore," she said, "I thought she should just pull herself together. And I really was going to need her to step up to the plate and take on more responsibility, and I wondered if that was going to be possible, with all this emotional stuff going on."

Chrissy fit the picture of the good worker who's suddenly pummeled by life events. She knew she was feeling anxious, sad, and stressed out; though she projected a sense of insecurity and looked to her boss for reassurance, she took accountability for her issues. Her job performance wasn't, as yet, affected. This category of the troubled subordinate does include basically healthy, action-oriented problem solvers and good performers. Chrissy could benefit from her boss's guidance, but Mary Ellen had fallen into the trap of responding to her assistant in the role of a comforting parent.

Concerning boss-to-subordinate relationships, the most common conflict I hear is the one I've just described, when a manager, out of genuine but misguided kindness, slides from the correct role of supportive coach into the incorrect role of parent or counselor. And once you succumb to the emotional demands of a troubled subordinate, you cannot be an effective manager. Begin to set limits by appreciating the difference between coaching and counseling:

In *coaching*, the goal is to improve a subordinate's performance and behavior through positive motivation.

In *counseling*, the goal is to explore the subordinate's feelings, including underlying causes of behavior. While certainly worthwhile, that is an effort that should occur more appropriately in a mental health professional's office than in a business office.

The internal reality piece: a diagnostic questionnaire

If you're smack in the middle of a Chrissy-type situation, the first step is to figure out if, how, and why you might have contributed to the time-consuming dilemma.

- **What am I feeling towards my troubled subordinate who is going through a rough time outside of work?**

    Would you identify those feelings as ones of guilt? Of worry?

    Do you feel a need to solve her problems?

    Have you been overindulgent?

    Are you becoming annoyed by her emotional neediness?

    This is where a blind spot often reveals itself, and, again, it might have a great deal to do with one's own parenting instincts. Mary Ellen was a case in point.

    She didn't have children herself. Interestingly, however, she had in a real sense parented her eight-years-younger sibling for a long time. "When I was in my early 20s, my sister Maggie was sort of falling apart. Depressed, sleeping all the time, barely getting to school. Our parents didn't have a clue what to do with her, and there were huge fights at home. So Maggie would come and stay with me sometimes." The sister eventually finished school, found a job and a small apartment, but the depression continued. "When she was about 21, 22," Mary Ellen said, "she started threatening suicide. She'd call me in the middle of the night and I'd spend three hours on the phone with her, just talking her through stuff."

That story had a happy ending. Maggie got on more solid ground over time, settled into a decent career and marriage, and the two sisters were able to enter into an adult-to-adult, mutually respectful, friendly relationship. Vestiges of that old way of connecting, however, when Mary Ellen was a surrogate mother to her sister, surfaced in her office dealings with stressed-out and unhappy Chrissy.

- ## How have I contributed to the way my subordinate is behaving?

That question comes down to this: Have I been more of a counselor or a parent than a coach? It is all too easy, almost without seeing it happen, to become an enabler—listening to the long stories, focusing on the subordinate's personal unhappiness or troubles, being soothing.

"I realized I'd made some big mistakes there," Mary Ellen said. "This very sweet girl, my assistant, had come to see me as her life support. I felt sorry for her, but I didn't have the time or the energy to give her anymore, though clearly I had sort of encouraged all that." She resolved to pull back, analyze the situation more carefully, and then figure out how to act towards her assistant less like a concerned mother and more like a manager, concentrating on helping ensure her effectiveness on the job.

The external reality piece: a diagnostic questionnaire

Before you can decide just how you'll begin the process of easing out of a counselor role, take a clear look at the externals.

- ### Is my troubled subordinate having a performance problem?

    There might not be one, as yet. But over the days or weeks to come, as you move your manager/subordinate relationship onto other grounds, it's crucial to keep an eye on whether the work is getting done in a timely and effective manner. Catch early any warning signs of deteriorating performance.

- ### Are my job expectations for my subordinate realistic?

    If the work environment involves a tidal wave of responsibilities, limited resources, or overwhelming deadlines, the employee who's stressed by personal events gets more stressed. When a talented subordinate who is not exhibiting performance problems starts reacting with emotional burnout, you might have added to her burdens through unrealistic expectations—for example, by asking her to work on multiple overlapping projects without adequate support.

    Mary Ellen needed to ask herself: Have I been pushing my assistant too hard at a time when she's experiencing family worries, roommate problems, and financial fears?

Best next steps

Mary Ellen regained control of her out-of-kilter manager/subordinate situation by taking the following steps.

- ### Move the counseling relationship out of your office.

    This effort begins with a pleasant, empathetic talk between manager and employee. When no performance problem exists, the talk can take the tone of a chat and an expression of encouragement.

Do not make your subordinate feel like a failure. A pressured individual who is a good worker should sense the need for emotional support is legitimate, and not a sign of weakness or a cause for personal shame.

Here are the ideas to convey:

1. You appreciate that she's having some difficulties, you are not unsympathetic; neither was she wrong to share her worries with you.
2. However, you are not trained to be, nor should you be, in a counseling role with her; better to get such help from people who provide counseling for a living.
3. You will be able point her in useful directions.

So Mary Ellen might say to Chrissy something like this:

"We value you, you've been doing a fine job. I am concerned about the problems you're facing; I know you're going through a very rough time. I hope that won't impact your work here, and I hope you'll get the support you need. I think it might be most effective if you can talk to a professional; I can make arrangements for you to call our corporate-sponsored employee assistance program. They can provide you with short-term counseling and maybe a referral for longer term if you need it, so you can get real help dealing with some of these issues. We can look over the benefit plan together, if you'd like more information on the available programs." (Information on employee assistance appears on page 78.)

If there is no corporate sponsored employee assistance resource, call HR before you have the meeting with your subordinate and ask what referrals they can provide. Then you can say to your employee, "I have some information from HR. I did not disclose to them who you are, but I've learned from them the names of some community organizations that we know of and that have excellent reputations. It might be a good idea to check these out."

The goal is to make your subordinate feel more effective, compliment her on her value, underscore how empathetic you are, suggest an avenue of help, and start moving the counseling relationship out of your office.

- ### Indicate that the subordinate is responsible for getting appropriate help.

    Going to employee assistance or a community service program is usually not mandatory, and a troubled subordinate might very well say that's the last thing she wants to do. Many employees dislike using corporate-sponsored resources, and depending on the organization or the reputation of the resource, that might be for a good reason. The manager still must convey the message—and perhaps more than once—that she's concerned and that she hopes her assistant is finding support elsewhere outside the company.

- ### Resist any inclination to become defensive.

    When you have essentially been parenting your employee, the emotional entanglements can run deep. Pulling back on the ever-available ear and the shoulder to cry on—trying to shift the relationship from parenting/counseling to managing/coaching—can feel hurtful to the assistant. Chrissy, for example, might very well say to her boss, "You used to be someone I could talk to," or in other ways show that she's feeling suddenly rebuffed.

    In that development, own up to the fact that out of a desire to be helpful and sympathetic, you did lend the shoulder to cry on. Acknowledge your culpability without becoming defensive about it.

    Mary Ellen might have to say to her assistant:

    "I understand you're feeling hurt and angry, because I did

encourage you to seek me out, and now I'm changing the rules on you. Please don't take this as a personal rejection. I still value and treasure you enormously, but my role as a manager is not to be a confidante. I'm sorry I raised those expectations and I acted in a way that causes you to feel hurt now, but I hope you know I was well-meaning. I also underestimated the tremendous pressure on my schedule [even if she has to fib about that a little], and my time is so limited now. I'm not abandoning you, I do care. But I think you'll get better, more consistent, and smarter help from professional counselors. And what I can do is maybe make your work life a bit easier."

- **Rearrange the subordinate's job assignments, if possible.**
    The external reality check will have revealed any of those unrealistic performance expectations, overloading of tasks, or other on-the-job demands that are making things worse for the troubled subordinate. Depending on her needs, increased time flexibility (that's usually welcomed if a family member is ill) or other practical adjustments might be a good idea.

EMPLOYEE ASSISTANCE PROGRAMS

- **What is employee assistance and what is it expected to do?**

    An employee assistance program (EAP) is a mental health service, sponsored by the organization—that provides a wide range of services—including short-term counseling, information about and referral to longer term treatment, and advice on family and financial issues and substance abuse. Some also do preretirement planning.

    The program might be internal, but most EAPs now tend to be external vendors that are contracted by the organization. They are made up of psychologists, social workers, and others with training

continued

in mental health issues, who will meet with an employee either on company premises or in their private offices.

• How and when might I get to EAP?

EAP is a place to go if you feel you're having personal pressures—family, financial, child care, substance use—that are disrupting your work, or if the office environment is impacting you psychologically to such an extent that you need to talk to someone for emotional support. They're there to provide information and to lessen your burden.

You can arrange a meeting yourself, without management knowing you've done so or what you're there to discuss. A directory of support services of the organization usually describes the existence of EAP or a hotline.

Management might also refer an employee. Typically, this happens when an employee is showing performance problems, and his boss is interested in keeping him in the job and wants to get him help. Management then might contact the EAP and let them know the reason for the referral. The employee might be told, "I think you might benefit from talking to these people and I'm setting up an appointment for you." What happens after that varies: The EAP professional might provide some feedback to management, or work in cooperation with HR to determine whether the employee should go on disability, or needs to be hospitalized or enter detox. EAP might be able, within limits of confidentiality, to give enough information to help HR and the boss to deal with the problem.

• Who pays for EAP support?

The organization pays. However, if you're referred for treatment outside the EAP, you are expected to pay for that yourself in conjunction with the mental health coverage in your benefits plan.

My first category of the troubled or troublesome subordinate—the temporarily stressed worker who is getting the job done but using her boss as an emotional security blanket—is in some ways the easiest to handle. The three categories coming up are trickier. For one thing, the inevitable talk is more of a confrontation than a chat. For another, once you're dealing with an employee whose difficulties are seriously interfering with performance, you usually can't go it alone—or rely solely on the advice I'm able to offer here.

If you find yourself in any of the scenarios I'm about to describe, check out what is available in your organization to help you manage your people—to help the manager manage. Assuming you have a supportive HR function with expertise in employee relations, reach out to them. Any of these situations just might end up in the inescapable need to fire the subordinate, and before taking that step you must make sure you have covered all the bases regarding company policies.

Manager Robert's story: what happened to him one day on the job

Robert was a vice president in a multifaceted organization in the entertainment business, a company that was committed to expansion through experimental new ventures. Robert was handed the assignment of designing and trying to place a series of small children's museums-cum-playspaces.

Given carte blanche to pick the talent he needed, Robert was delighted with the small staff he assembled, all gathered from divisions within the company. "I had a couple of excellent engineers who'd been involved in similar start-ups before," he said, "a good supply person, a good writer and PowerPoint woman who'd be responsible for our presentations to the company brass." Robert had particularly high hopes for Mark, a young man who hadn't been with the organization long, but who pitched himself for the job through a series of comic-book like illustrations depicting his talents. "He seemed to have the kind of mind that would work with this job, I thought he'd get what appealed to kids."

All went well at the start. Better than well, in fact. In meetings, Mark was a "Roman candle," his boss said, "He's shooting off ideas. Sometimes it was amazing what he'd come up with. The others thought he was terrific, a real inspiration and design guy." Mark came in with sketches for interactive exhibits that could be produced inexpensively, with innovative displays that combined science education and playtime, even with an idea for creating an imitation tropical rain forest, so visitors could experience the feeling of standing in a jungle.

A few months into the assignment, the picture was less rosy. Mark was missing deadlines and overlooking crucial steps for which he was responsible. He often showed up late for those meetings at which he could be so brilliant; when there, he sometimes seemed unfocused, his mind elsewhere. Mark had little patience when asked to toe the line in one way or another, and the others were starting to worry that keeping to their tightly imposed schedule was looking difficult.

What was Robert's reaction to these developments? He was aware of Mark's inconsistent behavior and performance and was frustrated by it. Basically, however, he preferred to ignore his bright young designer if he possibly could. He'd rather not have to deal with all the negative issues that came with the managerial package. After an informal progress report session one morning, he heard one of his engineers remark to another, "Well, Mark is the little can-do-no-wrong pet around here." It began to dawn on Robert that his own reputation as manager was being damaged.

Quite likely, Mark was a man with an apparent disorder or disability of some kind. His behavior—the inconsistency, the disorganization, the all-or-nothing extremes—is typical of brilliant workers who might be suffering from an attention deficit issue. They are often outstanding individual contributors according to their own time frames, which is why many of them make better entrepreneurs than corporate employees. A gifted, erratically performing employee might also be impaired by other clinical symptoms, including substance abuse and mental health problems, such as depression and anxiety.

The Marks of the business world are more problematic for managers than are the Chrissies. Their performance might be affected in a progressive and increasingly worsening way, as they exhibit patterns of tardiness, procrastination, frequent absenteeism, missed deadlines, mistakes, bad judgment, emotional outbursts, isolation, withdrawal, or impatience.

Denial might be present, but often these people ultimately do take responsibility for a decline in performance. Generally, they can be motivated to seek help, especially if they're given some warning of declining performance and are leveraged to seek assistance.

The internal reality piece: a diagnostic questionnaire

- **What are my feelings towards my subordinate whose performance is going down the tubes?**

  Imagine you have a child whose teachers are always telling you your child is not working up to his potential. (Maybe you do have such a child!) You know how smart he is, you know he could be bringing home all A's—and sometimes he does get an A, but then there's a D the next day. Or a report comes from school that says he failed to turn in an assignment on time or he's doing too much daydreaming during class.

  Are you angry? Or frustrated?

  Do you feel it's time to crack down?

  Faced with a troublesome subordinate who is capable of great things but not delivering on that potential in a consistent and expected way, you're likely to experience any range of emotions along these lines.

- ### Am I acting on parenting instincts that add to my subordinate's problem?

Have you been giving your troublesome child/subordinate an angry tongue-lashing? ("Just shape up!")

Or are you saying nothing, head in the sand, hoping that matters will magically improve themselves? This was manager Robert's blind spot.

Robert was the father of three sons, ranging in age from 10 to 16. His was a "traditional" family: Robert went to work and earned the money they lived on, his wife did not work outside the home and assumed the primary parenting role. The three boys were not "easy" kids, complete with messy rooms, dillydallying over homework, outbursts of disobedience, and so on. Their mother handled all child-related issues, and Robert was perfectly happy to let her do so. Ignoring troublesome behavior was his style.

At the office, his growing realization that the team he so valued was not working in great harmony any longer, that his own skill as a manager was being questioned, and that there was a danger of missing the assignment deadline—all this forced Robert to stop ignoring the problems with Mark. Robert had not been autocratic or overindulgent, but simply neglectful. To his credit, he was able to make the mental connection between the behaviors of Robert the manager and Robert the father.

"My wife deals with the kids," he said. "I take myself off the hook, I guess, by telling myself I work long hours, I've got a demanding job, and she handles the boys."

Clearly, that might describe his attitude toward Mark, and it was leading everybody into trouble. Mark's performance as a creative, "Roman candle" type was exceptional; his behavior in his corporate citizen role was poor and getting worse. "Once I realized what was going on, I started to get really frustrated and annoyed with Mark, because he's so bright and so creative, but he's just not reliable. He's not a bad guy, though he's obviously got some problems." Robert conducted a little due diligence.

The external reality piece: a diagnostic questionnaire

• Is my troublesome subordinate overloaded with work?

Assume that you might be somewhat responsible for your subordinate's poor behavior.

Are your work demands and expectations exacerbating the situation? If it turns out that, you realize, you've been putting this employee under 24/7 pressure for months, it's possible that easing his job requirements slightly will eliminate or diminish the performance problem.

• Am I giving my subordinate enough supervision?

Especially when a subordinate is involved in a team project, it can be easy to take it for granted that all participants are working at the same level—that the rising tide will carry all boats. And then it's easy to overlook the fact that one team player might require extra managerial attention.

Robert needed to think over his recent interactions with Mark: Was he keeping appropriate tabs on Mark's work in a nonjudgmental way?

• Where, exactly, is my subordinate falling down on the job?

A manager who's been guilty of ignoring the warning signs of deteriorating performance must get his radar functioning again and become extremely watchful. Document the employee's behaviors, take notes, and write down dates if relevant. Knowing he was going to have to talk to Mark sooner or later, Robert would be wise to prep himself by drawing up a short list of specific examples of where, when, and how the work had been inadequate.

- **What does the company have available to help me be a better manager?**

Are you aware of what your organization can provide in the way of managerial support? If not, this is the time to find out.

Best next steps

Before any kind of discussion with the subordinate takes place, cover your flank, do your homework, get information, go in prepared. A good starting point:

- **Alert your superior.**

Any manager of an impaired subordinate whose work is falling off really needs to clue in his own boss to the fact that a problem exists. That's just a smart managing-up strategy, because the last thing you want is for a deteriorating situation to reflect bad management on your part.

Robert, for example, might go to his boss and say: "I want you to know I'm on top of something that's happening in our group, and I'm going to try to get some counsel on how to handle it. You might have some ideas, so let me just fill you in a little on the situation, and tell me what you think." Not only do you protect yourself; cluing in your superior enhances your position, because you appear as someone in control and taking a proactive stance. Of course, listen to any suggestions he makes.

- **Seek informed advice.**

Robert wasn't a trained psychologist. He didn't know exactly what he was looking at, in fact, but just thought Mark was unmotivated or careless, or a guy with "some problems." Before he could choose an appropriate solution, he needed advice.

Dealing with an impaired subordinate is a tricky business, and an enlightened HR professional can be helpful. In addition to the services discussed previously, HR people can advise a manager about specific corporate policies, such as corrective action processes, and coach about the right language to use when discussing a troublesome situation privately with the subordinate. These staff employees are usually familiar with the fact that some highly gifted workers also come with the kinds of erratic and disorganized behaviors that Mark displayed, and that an attention disorder is a realistic possibility. However, a manager, or anyone in the company, cannot suggest to an employee that he might have ADD, a disability, because it is illegal for an organization to diagnose anyone in that manner (nor should a manager offer the opinion that his worker has mental problems, a drinking problem—unless there's obvious drinking on the job—a depression problem, or anything of the sort. This, too, is diagnosing, and diagnosing is off limits in this context).

But, this same informed HR professional might suggest interventions that are legal, ethical, and humane, including employee assistance programs and corporate sponsored coaching and training.

• **Talk with the subordinate.**

Again, it's crucial to avoid any hint of diagnosing an ailment or disability. Here is the general script to follow:

1. Express appreciation for the subordinate's talents and contribution, and avoid shaming him in any way. Do not go on the attack or sound judgmental. Do not try to discuss causes of poor behavior, unless the employee introduces the subject.

2. Describe how his difficult behavior has manifested and the consequences on performance. In other words, point out that some aspects of how he's doing his job are not going well, and present fact-based information on what those are.

3. Suggest that the behaviors need to be modified, and that it is his responsibility to do so. Tell him that you will help him in that effort. But make it clear that the behavior must change immediately, and if it doesn't, his job could be in jeopardy. It's important to keep notes on this discussion, recording both the date and the content, and place the recorded information in a safe, confidential place. The purpose of this note taking is to be prepared in case the behavior does not improve and further action needs to be taken. The notes serve as a reminder.

So Robert, for example, might say to Mark in a private meeting in his office: "Look, you're an exceptional person, you've done great things here and come up with wonderful ideas. At the same time, however, there's been a consistent pattern of unreliability over several months. Let me tell you how that has been demonstrated. You've arrived late to three of our last four departmental meetings, you missed the deadline for your last status report, your office looks like a disaster area, and you haven't kept others informed in the way we outlined. This reflects badly on you. You're such a creative guy and such a good performer, that I don't like to see this happening."

Once it's been made absolutely clear that something's got to change, manager and subordinate can discuss possibilities, with the manager making suggestions he will implement. And again, a man like Mark—when he understands that his good qualities are noticed and valued—is likely to be receptive and to appreciate that it's in his best interests to work at getting his act together.

- **Rearrange the subordinate's tasks.**

If the external reality check revealed that this talented but troublesome subordinate is being overloaded or asked to take on tasks he's not particularly good at, improve that picture as far as is realistic and possible. This is a further demonstration that you, the manager, are willing to do your part in helping your employee be more effective, and you've given some thought to how you'll accomplish that.

Robert might tell Mark, "What I'd like to do is share certain responsibilities between the two of us. It's clear that these more administrative duties are not your forte. I'd like to reduce some of these things, and here's how it will work." Robert then outlines the two or three routine paperwork tasks for which Mark will no longer have to be responsible.

- **Increase contact time.**

In addition to decreasing some of the pressures, set up increased face-to-face time. More actively managing a gifted but impaired subordinate whose performance is getting wobbly is an excellent way to impose structure and also positively motivate him to reform.

For example, if Mark knows that henceforth once a week, every Monday morning or Friday afternoon, Robert will be stopping by his office to get a briefing on what Mark has been up to, Mark has an organizational plan to his work life that he's had trouble coming up with himself.

- **Suggest corporate-sponsored coaching/training services, as well as provide referrals to employee assistance.**

Many companies use internal or external professional coaches with various specialties to work with valued employees for behavioral modification or skill development. (See the box on coaching, on page 90.) Typically, the coach, after meeting with the manager and the employee, assesses what interventions are necessary to improve the employee's effectiveness. Someone like Mark could benefit enormously from three to six months of coaching support, which would help him develop awareness of his problem and his behaviors, and gain better time and office management skills.

In addition to coaching, Mark's boss can refer him to an employee assistance program, easing him into it by saying: "The coaching and my efforts might be helpful, but you might need to explore whether your performance problems reflect other underlying issues that require other professional help."

Both referrals at this point are voluntary, but the warning is still real.

• Keep tabs on the subordinate's progress.

Once a referral is made, your work isn't done. You need to monitor your subordinate's performance and observe whether or not there's progress. Offer praise when positive changes are appearing.

Just keep tabs on how things are going. When this worker receives a combination of support—possibly outside therapy and medication, suggestions from a coach or organizational consultant, more contact time with the manager—problems usually will decrease.

The key here: When your subordinate is someone who's performing reasonably well and you suspect his growing difficulties on the job are related to medical or psychological issues, intervene as early as you can. You don't want symptoms to lead to the third category, described below, when significant and destructive performance problems appear.

COACHING

• What is involved in coaching?

Coaching is a one-on-one service in which a professional coach works with an employee. There are three general categories or specialties:

1. In behavioral coaching, the aim is to modify the employee's behaviors to fit a particular job and find a better adjustment within the work environment. A behavioral coach typically has a business and mental health background or experience.
2. In leadership/development coaching, the goal is to help the employee expand skills, such as communication in media appearances, and enhance his general effectiveness in a managerial or leadership role. These coaches usually have both business background and some training in teaching skill building.
3. Career coaches work with people who are thinking about changing careers or help to find the right fit between personal talents and interests and the job world. Similar to career counseling, this kind of coaching helps the individual actualize professional goals by evaluating skills, sometimes through assessment tests, and exploring job possibilities. Career coaches generally have an excellent understanding of the marketplace regarding different kinds of jobs and the skills they require.

• Do I find a coach myself or does the company send me to one?

Some coaching is corporate sponsored; some is "retail"—you'll locate a coach to work with and pay for the service yourself.

More and more organizations are committed to coaching, which might be provided either internally, sometimes by trained HR personnel, or through external professionals. Coaching is usually offered only to valued employees or people with high potential.

continued

This is an employee who might have outstanding expertise or knowledge, but some skill gaps, behavioral rough edges, or inadequate interpersonal strengths. Or, it's an employee who accepts the responsibility and the challenge of improving and expanding his skill set, and moving up the organizational hierarchy through the appropriate training. Coaching is not often offered to an employee with performance problems whom the company is not particularly interested in keeping.

In corporate sponsored coaching, the company pays, even if they use external coaches. Behavioral or leadership/development coaching might last for three to six months, sometimes a year.

You might decide you need and want the benefit of coaching, either to hone certain skills to be more effective in your job or to explore other career possibilities entirely. If it's not available to you through your organization, consider arranging for it privately.

Ask friends for a referral, perhaps a friend who works for a company that does sponsor coaching. You can also do Internet searches that might list executive coaches and/or career counselors in your geographical location. Interview the coach over the phone to ask about background and experience.

Manager Bill's story: what happened to him one day on the job

Bill worked in a brokerage house, in charge of a division researching and selling new technologies for the financial industry. When Bill moved up to a more senior position, he appointed his subordinate Don as division manager, reporting to Bill as before and now also overseeing the work of about a dozen associates. Little did Bill realize at the time that he had created a Dr. Jekyl and Mr. Hyde out of his ambitious, hard-working subordinate.

Don was an outstanding salesperson who managed his customers well and was unfailingly supportive towards Bill, his boss. Once he became a manager of others, his less attractive and in fact maladaptive behaviors emerged. Being a perfectionist and demanding, Don drove his staff mercilessly. When his people didn't live up to what were basically unrealistic expectations, he was outraged; he yelled about mistakes and had temper tantrums. In general, he showed contempt for the less powerful employees in his path.

Don was an example of the subordinate with a personality disorder, an individual who because of personal qualities behaves badly and creates wide dysfunction and unrest in the work environment. Like many in this category, he could be friendly and engaging when managing up; his problems came to the fore in managing down. In that role, he was perceived as, and was, autocratic and abusive.

Bill was largely unaware of the misery Don was creating, until two developments took place. First, complaints about Don were being registered with HR. "Harassment" was mentioned. Second, Don's managing-up behavior took a worrisome turn. Bill heard through the grapevine that Don had initiated a couple of lunch dates with the division VP who was *Bill's* boss. He had no reason to suspect anything underhanded was going on, but the idea of his subordinate and his boss having lunch, with neither mentioning the fact to him, didn't sit well.

So Bill decided to say something to Don, and dropped by his office one afternoon. "How's everything going in your department, Don?" he said. "I hear you've been kind of cracking the whip around here." Don's reply was that he was finally getting some real work out of a bunch of malingerers and bringing the department up to par.

Subordinates with personality disorders are one of the most difficult, if not the most difficult employees to manage. They might be immature, dependent employees who continually expect to be taken care of; passive aggressive individuals, who comply on one hand and then sabotage or resist on the other; rigid people, like Don, who expect perfection from themselves and from everyone who works for them; narcissists who need to be the center of attention and exploit others to that end; or cold and aloof individuals who treat coworkers in a mechanical way. There's also the opportunist, a kind of sociopath, who seeks power and is unethical—who sabotages his underlings by taking credit for their accomplishments, lies and distorts information for his own benefit, or misuses expense accounts.

But these people often sail right through the hiring process. Character and personality disorders can go unnoticed at initial screening and recruiting time, because such employees are often charming, even chameleon-like. Once on the job, however, and once maladaptive behaviors start appearing, they're particularly troublesome because they typically assume no responsibility for their actions. Behaving badly, they're not necessarily in psychic pain of their own. In fact—and here's where the manager faces a real challenge in any attempts to control or change behavior—they often deny having any problems at all. When confronted, they'll blame the environment, present themselves as victims, or in other ways fail to acknowledge or even recognize how their actions are contributing to a miserably negative environment.

When dealing with this individual, don't do it alone. In this situation, the advice and support of HR is crucial.

The internal reality piece: a diagnostic questionnaire

- **How do I feel about my subordinate's havoc-creating behavior?**
     Are you baffled by it?
     Disbelieving?
     Upset?

Once Bill became aware of some of the antagonism and unhappiness Don was stirring up in his department, his immediate feeling was one of confusion. He was puzzled. Don was his star performer, delivering so well, bringing in new business and turning in outstanding and fresh research. In short, Don was a delightful guy. What was going on?

Any such surprising emotions might be present. It's as if the child who is his parents' pride and joy, ace student, top grades, polite and respectful to all grown-ups, turns out to be a bully on the school playground and lunchroom, pushing around the little kids.

• How am I responding to my subordinate in the face of my feelings?

When a troublesome subordinate is acting in really bad ways—immorally, unethically, illegally—a manager can feel betrayed and enraged. You might wish to punish him, get him out of the way as fast as possible, and throw him in jail. Punitive reactions or a desire for revenge are not uncommon, but it's important to cool down. Never take action or set up a confrontation when you're angry or caught up in those powerful emotions.

Bill's initial response was somewhat the opposite. Like a puzzled, befuddled parent whose child is seemingly acting not like himself, Bill's blind spot was to detach from the whole problem. He became a little paralyzed—letting the situation drift, becoming independent from it, assuming his overall positive experience with Don would serve everyone well in the end.

When serious complaints started coming in, however, he began to worry about the potential for litigation, which could damage his own position and reputation. And then when Bill got a whiff of the fact that Don was doing end-runs around him, going over his head to Bill's boss, he became angry as well. Bill knew he had to take action and confront his employee.

The external reality piece: a diagnostic questionnaire

- ### Is my subordinate's behavior typical of others in this environment?

If so, how are they being managed?

This is a key question. In some corporate cultures, aggressive, demanding, autocratic, even verbally abusive behaviors on the part of a manager towards the people he's in charge of are not that unusual. But there are extremes, and in every organization some extremes are unacceptable. It's necessary for Bill to figure out where Don fits within that range.

Bill had been with his firm for many years. He was familiar with the various departments and the people in them, and he knew that humane and considerate managing down was an important value. Don's behavior was not typical of the place, and was not encouraged or rewarded.

- ### Do I have the full story of what's going on?

What more information might you need?

Again, careful, specific fact gathering is in order. Here are some questions you might need to answer:

What has been the nature of complaints to HR (if any)?

What are people around the office saying?

What is the makeup of the group my troublesome subordinate is managing? If it's a diverse population—men and women, racially or culturally mixed—the subordinate's bad behavior is potentially even more threatening to the organization.

It's not always easy to pick up a consistent pattern right away. It might be necessary to be even a little sly as you conduct your due diligence—because employees with the kinds of personality defects I've described are often quite smart, wiley, and self-protective. You might not hear outright complaints, but simply realize you are suspicious; you have a gut feeling that something's fishy, or that you're being sabotaged. Maybe there's an expense account that looks wrong; maybe you learn of an unethical request the subordinate has made of one of his employees.

Other information-gathering possibilities: In some organizations—not all—a manager is encouraged to do "two down," or go two levels below, meeting with the employee or employees who report to the subordinate, and conducting interviews to determine the quality and tone of work-life in that office. Some companies use what is called a "360," an annual survey that assesses performance, behavior, and reputation by asking questions of the bosses, the peers, and the subordinates. The results are rated and usually summarized in some form of a report. The 360 is a useful tool, because the information is gathered through a confidential and anonymous process.

Armed with information you've obtained in any of these ways, you're ready to explore and implement solutions.

Best next steps

• Get appropriate internal advice and support.

Such advice can come from HR, the legal department, or another department within the organization that is familiar with employee law. Go there.

Bill might say to this helpful individual: "Don, for the most part, is performing his job, and he's delivering on his goals. But part of his job is managing people, and I'm aware that he's forcing them to work extremely hard, his expectations might be unrealistic and they're certainly badly conveyed. His staff is complaining about him; they feel harassed and abused, the complaints are serious, and I have potential litigation on my hands. So I'm convinced this is a serious performance problem on his part. What's the protocol? How do we handle somebody like this?"

One piece of information that might be gleaned is whether or not the troublesome subordinate can be fired immediately because of bad behavior. If the behavior is unethical or illegal, possibly he can be fired. On the other hand, manipulative behavior—like Don making end-runs around Bill and talking to Bill's boss—or simply unpleasant behavior is probably not grounds for dismissal.

Again, an informed internal advisor will be able to outline corporate policies and describe the appropriate steps to take next.

• Cover any necessary bases with your boss.

Here's a scenario you want to avoid: Your subordinate's behavior gets worse or veers into the downright illegal, or one of the abused employees initiates a legal action, matters come to a boil, you fire the subordinate, and your boss says, "What happened here? Why didn't I know about any of this?" Head any such possibility off at the pass by letting your own supervisor know that there's a tricky situation among your employees, and you're taking steps to handle it.

Bill had the added problem of a subordinate apparently cozying up to the boss's boss. And he might not be entirely sure that the big boss didn't somewhat feed into that situation, enjoying the opportunity to do a little spying or get inside information. Taking all this into consideration, Bill might approach his boss and say something like this: "You know, Don is a very useful employee, he's smart, but I think he's getting kind of big-headed about his relationship with you, and that's somewhat interfering with my position as his manager. Would you do me a favor? If there's information you need that he's involved in, come to me and ask me for it? That empowers my position here."

You do not want to tell the senior boss he can't do something; you're just asking for his help and cooperation in a politically astute manner. Get the boss off the hook.

Then, too, Bill should certainly let his subordinate know that he's on to his bit of manipulative behavior, by saying casually, "Hey Don, it's come to my attention that you've had lunches with my boss Frank on a couple of occasions. Fine, I'm glad that you've been able to establish your presence around here. However, there are certain basic, corporate citizen, respectful things you should do, and one is to alert me if there's anything in the conversations you're having with Frank that pertains to me and that I need to be sensitive to. That's good subordinate behavior, and I would expect that from you."

- **Initiate a discussion with the subordinate.**
  Here are the key concepts to the initial talk you'll have:

  1. Don't start a war. Don't go on the attack. Be diplomatic.
  2. Do not at this juncture offer assistance or help, unless the subordinate takes some accountability for his behavior.
  3. Let your employee know that you're requesting behavioral change on his part, and you will be evaluating whether or not that occurs.

For example, Bill might say to Don, in a private conversation: "Look, you're obviously intelligent and productive; you and I have a good working relationship. I appreciate the value you've added to our business. But I'm concerned about problems with your behavior that are impacting your performance. We're in a culture where managers are expected to be good coaches to their people. And according to the reports I've been getting, you're not acting in that manner. You are described as being overly dictatorial; you have humiliated your people publicly. This is not the kind of management behavior that we can accept. We need you to make some adjustments because it's interfering with an important aspect of your job."

Now, ideally, the subordinate on the hot seat accepts your

explanation, understands your point, and acknowledges that he must improve his managing-down behavior. That might be a good time to bring up the possibility of a temporary period of coaching to help him in that effort.

However, be prepared for a reaction that is more typical of the blaming individual with a personality issue. This guy takes no accountability, accuses his staff of being overly sensitive prima donnas, people who don't know what real hard work is, and essentially lets you know he has no idea what you're talking about. He doesn't see any of what you have described as his problem.

If your employee responds in this way, shift your tone from kindly to more demanding, even a bit curt, but still calm and direct. For example: "Your behavior is out of line, and you simply can't get away with it any longer. You need to speak to people differently. I'm concerned that if this is not modified, it will affect your career."

• Document your conversation.

This is when you, the manager, could start getting into hairy situations with real trouble looming. Even if the talk has seemingly gone well—your employee took responsibility and resolved to improve—document the conversation just passed: what you said, what he said, what was agreed upon. Such a record, which you keep for yourself, might be important as developments proceed. If the talk went *badly*, it might be time to update your HR or legal department contact, and get further advice.

• Address your subordinate again, with a warning this time.

Let's assume that Don sat silently as Bill delivered his suggestions, replied with some version of "I don't think I have a problem," and left without any reassurances to his boss that he got the picture.

What's more: After that conversation, he went back to work and retaliated on his staff, with more criticism and flares of temper.

Bill might have to take a further step and put Don on a more formal warning. So he says: "I haven't seen improvement. Whatever you believe, the bottom line is, your behavior is not acceptable within this organization. Your response to my feedback was not satisfactory. You have some talents, but you're not going to be able to continue in this position if your actions with your staff don't change. You have three months to show improvement."

• Remain vigilant.

As is true in any scenario concerning a troubled or troublesome subordinate, your managerial function isn't over once you've had the talk and pointed out what needs to be done. You can only judge how successful you've been if in a few days, weeks, or months it's clear the desired improvements have taken place—and if they stick as time goes on. But especially if you're sitting on a situation including the prospect of litigation, it's crucial that you keep the radar up and track what's happening, or what's not happening.

When a subordinate doesn't "own" his problem, when he denies any responsibility for difficulties he has in fact created, there is a probability he might be fired. That probability also exists if he does accept responsibility, but fails to improve. He might even have received help in the form of external counseling advice, changed his behaviors accordingly, and yet after a brief time the old patterns reemerge and he reverts back to the kinds of actions that got him in trouble in the first place.

Don was an example of the first response. The warning made little impact; his deadline came and went. Consequently, with the help of HR, Bill managed Don out of the company. This subordinate's behavioral pattern was just not a good fit for the organization.

Manager Vincent's story: what happened to him one day on the job

Vincent, 55, was a regional supervisor for a national firm that provided private tutoring for students with learning difficulties. Based in a suburban area outside New York City, Vincent was in charge of three centers that attracted children from elementary through the high-school grades, who were signed up by parents for one-on-one remedial help in reading and math, small groups for social skills coaching, precollege testing preparation, and other services. Business was booming. And Vincent gave himself credit for that degree of success, because he hired only the best employees he could find.

One of his star performers was Eleanor, a 35-year-old reading specialist who demonstrated great results with young students. As the business continued to grow, Vincent eventually employed eight full-time reading specialists, who worked either on site at one or another of the centers, or at students' schools after-hours. Wanting to maintain an overall approach to the work and a greater measure of centralized control, he promoted Eleanor to a newly created position as chief of the reading tutors. She'd still work with her students, but in addition she would maintain contact with the others in her specialty—coordinate efforts, communicate any general directives from the boss, and so on.

This wasn't a particularly onerous task. Actually, Vincent mainly wanted his employees to have the sense of being part of a team, whose members knew each other and felt they were working under the same umbrella—especially since Vincent himself wasn't easily available. At their monthly meeting, Vincent told the group about the new arrangement, and everyone was actually quite pleased about it. The others didn't know that much about Eleanor, but thought she was an amiable person. They saw value in the idea of having one appointed go-to person, someone they could approach concerning a snag or a success in their work with clients and get feedback, maybe suggestions on how others handled particular problems. In fact, most expressed the opinion that this central coordination had been a missing piece in the picture. It was agreed that in the future, Eleanor would be in charge of setting up the monthly meetings.

Three months later, Vincent was starting to hear gripes. A couple of his employees waited to catch him before he left his office; a couple of others reached him by phone in the evenings. Eleanor, it turned out, was largely invisible. When Eleanor was at the center on the same day as some of the other specialists, she stayed closeted in her office. She didn't walk around to see how things were going or say hello, she never communicated in person, and she rarely talked. She was a little better at replying to e-mails, but not much. In addition, since the new arrangement had been put in place, there had been no monthly meeting scheduled. "Vincent," one of his employees said, "you're the busiest guy around here, but it was always easier to reach you than to reach her."

Eleanor was an example of a solid performer as an individual contributor, who was suddenly out of her element once promoted to a management role. Her behavior was not nasty, dictatorial, or unpleasant. She was just not there—somewhat detached; unresponsive to, uncomfortable with, or maybe unaware of the "people skills" her new role demanded.

This category of troublesome subordinate includes employees who do not display major distress or disorders, who might be highly competent in areas of technical expertise and knowledge, but have rough edges. They lack good interpersonal skills, empathy towards others, or generally speaking, "emotional intelligence." Managers typically do want to retain these people because of their talents. Vincent certainly didn't want to lose Eleanor. What to do about the Eleanor problem, however, was stumping him. He needed to think over the situation.

The internal reality piece: a diagnostic questionnaire

- ### **What are my feelings toward this competent subordinate who's no good at interacting with everybody else?**

Typically, your primary feeling might be one of disappointment. You had high hopes for a respected employee, and then found those hopes were not realized.

Or do you feel annoyed with yourself for moving your subordinate into a more demanding position, and think you made a big mistake?

Are you inclined to be protective towards this individual, as you would toward a shy, socially inept son or daughter? And a little impatient at the same time, wondering why this child can't just rise to reasonable social demands?

That described Vincent's reactions, in general. He was a fatherly man, proud of his talented staff and wanting everyone to feel part of a big, happy family. And he certainly didn't want to hurt Eleanor's feelings by telling her she wasn't working out in the new spot. But he did want her to recognize her shortcomings and do something about them.

The external reality piece: a diagnostic questionnaire

- ### **How exactly is my subordinate falling down on the job?**

Vincent took a more extensive survey among the individuals Eleanor was supposed to be leading, and his initial impressions were confirmed. She wasn't abusing anybody; she wasn't doing bad or wrongful things. She simply wasn't doing enough, wasn't engaged in a way that the position required.

He decided he had two options: bring Eleanor up to the task or demote her.

Best next steps

• Talk over the situation with the subordinate.

This will be a kindly and empathetic chat. Again, it's so important to be diplomatic. An employee should always feel valued for *something*; even if it's her longevity or a particular bit of work she's accomplished. When you express appreciation, you both reduce defensiveness and energize your worker to be motivated to change.

In Vincent's case, it was not difficult to highlight the positives in Eleanor's performance. His conversation with her might sound something like this: "I'm glad you're here today; we have some things to talk about. First, I want to underscore that I value the contributions you've made; you've really helped your clients achieve. Now this new position I've given you is a little more troublesome. I can understand that I'm asking you to do some things that weren't part of your job life before, when you were solely an individual contributor and focused on that task. Now you have to outreach to your coworkers, and for somebody who I think is probably kind of introverted, requiring you to engage with all the other specialists must be tough for you. But in this environment, that's something you need to learn."

Saying someone is introverted is probably safe; that's a description, not a diagnosis. And it is really a compassionate way of pointing out a common human vulnerability.

• Arrange for coaching.

It's not usually appropriate to refer this troublesome subordinate for counseling help, because there's no indication of emotional or medical problems. Neither is she a candidate for performance warnings. But she might be an ideal one for coaching and training to improve her competencies in the area of emotional intelligence, in order to complement her otherwise excellent performance. (See the sidebar on page 90 for further information on coaching)

Vincent told Eleanor: "I've talked to the head office, and they've agreed to support you through some management development training. I can arrange for a coach who'll find out more from your coworkers what you could be doing that will make them more effective, and then the coach will help you develop some basic skills in these areas."

Eleanor, who realized her limitations, was pleased with that offer.

• Redesign the subordinate's job.

Eleanor turned out to be a receptive, willing trainee; and her interaction skills improved significantly. That won't be the outcome in every case, however. Some employees are simply happiest and most effective as outstanding individual contributors, working largely alone and not required to supervise others. If that had been true for Eleanor, Vincent probably would have been wise to chalk up the promotion as a mistake and allow his excellent reading specialist to go back to doing what she did best.

In the four categories of the troubled or troublesome subordinate that I've described, several common elements pertain:

Let your conversation and actions reflect respect and value to the employee, even if he's extremely difficult and even if you're going to fire him.

Provide him with a chance to safely communicate his concerns. If he vents emotions or behaves badly, neither ignore nor overindulge.

Give candid, diplomatic, concrete information and feedback.

Make clear your expectations that it is up to him to manage his reactions and improve his behavior.

Offer referrals for counseling programs, coaching, or training, whatever seems to be an appropriate intervention.

Then follow up to determine if all has proceeded according to plan.

PART 2

SURVIVING CHANGE

A FEW FIRST THOUGHTS

The following two chapters concern the matter of change in the office, an occurrence that typically stirs up anxiety in the workers going through it and powerful feelings—of loss, anger, resentment, and fear.

No one really wholeheartedly embraces imposed, unwanted change in our places of employment. As long as life has been running smoothly, we'd all prefer that familiar routines and individuals remain the same, as we've come to know them. The danger is that stirred-up emotions and the acting-out behaviors they precipitate can cloud any effort—and it's a critical effort—to observe matters objectively, in order to make necessary adjustments or to realize it's time to move elsewhere. Perhaps more than in any other tricky workplace situation, you must face reality so that you do not end up a victim—that is, out of a job.

It helps to realize that although it might be uncomfortable, change per se isn't a bad thing. On the contrary, especially if well-managed by good leadership, change can feed the creative process in organizations and people, promoting greater success and optimal performance.

5

NEW MANAGEMENT

HOW TO ADAPT TO A SHIFTING CAST OF CHARACTERS

"New management" might arrive in one of two ways. One, your company has been acquired by or merged with another organization, a new senior team comes into position, and, possibly, large-scale operational or cultural shifts become apparent. Or two, your immediate supervisor leaves for another job, retires, or moves out of the picture in some other way, and you have a new boss to whom you're reporting, while the company as a whole remains essentially the same.

In either case, in all likelihood you will have to do some things you've always done in a different way; in an extreme situation, you might need to figure out how to fit yourself into a redesigned picture entirely. The psychological pressures can be enormously hard to manage.

In the scenarios that follow, we look at those two possibilities:

- Adapting to a new management team—and how employee Joan coped

- Adapting to a new supervisor—and how employee Frank coped

We'll assume here that the new regime or new boss has no intention of firing you because of downsizing or the decision to replace the existing staff in toto. (That's another story and another psychological pressure entirely.) Your job is not on the line, as long as you continue to perform effectively and meet the new world order in an appropriate and timely manner. The issue is all about dealing with unwanted change, and that's a matter that can bring out the best or worst in all of us. Whether it's the best or the worst or somewhere in between depends upon several factors: individual temperament, past patterns of coping, and how (or whether) the new regime or new supervisor helps in the process and the manner in which it delivers the change.

How those factors mesh explains a great deal about whether an individual experiences the situation as highly toxic or not too terrible after all.

We explore these variables in the experiences of Joan and Jack.

Joan's story: what happened to her one day on the job

Joan, 38, was an editor on the staff of a national monthly woman's magazine, a job she'd held and enjoyed for over twelve years. She had well-developed work habits, was respected for her talents and as a team player, and felt a high degree of comfort and belonging. Several strong friendships she'd made with other staff members were highly important to her. "A couple of people there were really like family to me," she said. "We kidded around a lot, but we also helped each other with the work." Joan was unmarried and without children, and this "second family" in the office added to her feelings of being part of a caring community.

Her work hours were relatively flexible. Two or three days each month, when an issue was going to press, it was often necessary for Joan and others to remain at work until ten or eleven at night. It was an accepted practice, then, to arrive at the office late in the morning at times when the workload was lighter. Joan liked that. "Nobody was looking over your shoulder all the time; you were trusted to do your job when the job had to get done. You felt you were recognized as a responsible person." Adding to her sense of comfort was an easygoing relationship with her boss, the editor-in-chief, a person with an open-door policy and a willingness to discuss snags or new ideas at any time.

The magazine was sold to a major international communications conglomerate, with headquarters in Europe. "Almost at once," Joan said, "everything changed." The editor-in-chief was replaced, and the replacement brought in two individuals who were installed in newly created positions. Long established ways of working, such as how copy was handled and how article ideas were presented, were replaced virtually overnight with different procedures as well as the new chain of command. "With this editor, you could no longer just stick your head in her office and ask a quick question or two," Joan said. "She really wanted all communication to go through the deputy and assistant deputy editors, these people we didn't have before. And they announced that we'd be having a weekly meeting to talk about progress. One of them sent out a memo that said, 'Here's what we're looking at—meetings, meetings, meetings!'" There would also be a twice-yearly, written and in-person performance reviews, "something we'd never had," Joan said. "Nobody used to think that was necessary."

In addition to these concrete differences in the way Joan would be expected to manage her job and would be judged on it, there were immediate signs, conveyed through e-mails and memos, that a cultural change was underway, with a focus on cost cutting and the bottom line. Editors were advised to keep their expense accounts down; staff members would be expected to share trade magazines and newspapers to which they previously held individual subscriptions; the editor-in-chief requested that "all staff please be in the office by 9 a.m. each morning." Under the old regime, the company had been, if not exactly paternalistic, clearly more generous—for one thing, demonstrating in the form of some of these small perks that employees were valued. A shift in spirit was palpable. The announced cancellation of the "day in the country," a long-established annual event each summer when the whole staff spent one weekday at a country club for sports and dinner didn't help morale among the long-term employees.

Joan was unhappy. When one of her favorite coworkers quit (she decided to leave the field entirely and become a partner in her sister's catering business), Joan's misery deepened.

Jack's story: what happened to him one day on the job

Jack, an attorney in his mid-40s, had been with his firm for five years. A corporate lawyer, he worked for a large organization in the health services field. The job suited Jack to a tee. He had an excellent relationship with his boss, the corporate general counsel. Although he reported on a monthly basis to the boss, Jack had an essentially autonomous job, running one of the divisions of the business, setting his own hours and other aspects of the work. He loved it. He'd always toyed with the idea of having his own practice as an attorney, and this job almost filled the bill—a corporate position, with the security that provided, but one he could maintain in a largely independent manner. His boss had a lot of confidence in him and also wasn't a particularly controlling individual.

More than that: The boss was aware of Jack's family situation, which for about a year had been highly unsettled. Jack was going through a bitter divorce that involved painful issues regarding custody of the couple's two young sons, and he was especially appreciative of his boss's sensitivity to his need to address himself to those matters.

Jack had to be available for court appearances, mandated home visits from family-court-appointed experts, and other time-consuming sessions. He was careful not to let all that interfere with his productivity on the job.

New management for Jack arrived in the form of a new supervisor, while the company went on as before.

Jack's boss, the man who'd hired him, retired suddenly and unexpectedly, and his position was taken by a new general counsel. This individual, it became clear to Jack very quickly, had a different management style. While previously individual attorneys responded to the business demands, reporting loosely, this general counsel's philosophy was that corporate should have more control over the attorneys. Day-to-day operations would not be as decentralized.

The boss wasn't mean; he just demanded greater responsiveness and "face time" than the old boss. For Jack, the fallout from such management change meant added paperwork, more meetings that involved all the associates, a demanding reporting relationship, and the need for a different approach to how he scheduled his day and managed his time. His work hours grew. Jack had a busier, more constricted job—while he still had to cope with the outside pressures from his personal life.

Jack got angry. He recognized, he said, "feeling so overwhelmed every day, everything is landing down on me at once. And it is mainly because this guy arrived pretty much out of the blue and changed all the rules. Like it or lump it."

One afternoon, because of a meeting he had to attend at work, Jack arrived late for a scheduled court-mandated mediation session with his wife. Already on edge, he lost his cool when the talk got underway and made outrageous accusations about his wife. "That was a stupid thing to do," he said. "It certainly didn't help my cause."

Changes in management—when those changes are unexpected,

unwanted, or imposed without your permission, consent, or willingness—will cause in just about anyone a decrease in feelings of security and an increase in feelings of anxiety. A sense of direction, belongingness, control, autonomy, and self-esteem, all can be powerfully affected.

Everyone will be shaken up to some degree and will face a process of adjustment that is not unlike mourning the death of a loved one. Obviously, the experience is not as devastating as a death in the family or among friends, but the emotions can be similar— sadness, denial, resistance, anger. How one goes through that, and the amount of psychic pain involved, is idiosyncratic. And that, in turn, is directly related to the internal and external realities in play.

Here's how to understand the interconnection.

- If you are particularly vulnerable to unwanted change, if that's where your blind spots lie *and* new management handles the transition poorly, or with little support and empathy, you might experience the process in a severe or elongated manner, with strong symptoms of sadness, anxiety, confusion, or helplessness, and self-defeating behaviors as well.

- If you are highly vulnerable to unwanted change *but* new management handles the shifting landscape in a respectful, helpful, and sophisticated way, you are likely to have an easier time with it.

- If you have essentially good and resilient coping mechanisms *but* new management shows no empathy and provides no help in the adjustment process—you're essentially thrown into the water and expected to sink or swim on your own— you might be in trouble.

- If you have no unusual blind spots *and* new management finesses the changes beautifully, you might experience only a modicum of the emotions and behaviors I'll describe.

Time to ferret out what's you, what's them, and how the two mesh.

We'll see now how Joan and Jack, dealing with different forms of management, fit the picture.

The internal reality piece: a diagnostic questionnaire

As always, the goal of a little thoughtful self-questioning is first, to identify your emotions, and second, to recognize how you're acting in the wake of those emotions.

To know if you might be particularly vulnerable to any kind of change, even if it's managed decently by those imposing it, ask yourself:

- **Do I have a history of painful past losses?**

Have you ever witnessed or been victimized by traumatic events? The death of a parent early in one's life, a home that burned down or had to be abandoned abruptly, any such long ago abrupt and difficult shift in life circumstances can be the trigger that reactivates feelings of anxiety when faced with a new instance of change and loss.

This was Joan's history, in fact. As a child, she had been through several major losses—the death of her father, the death of her older brother one year later, and the need for her mother and herself to live for a while after that with grandparents in a nearby state. Though she wasn't consciously mourning those events in adulthood, their psychological impact was still powerful. On the job, Joan disliked the removal of perks, the imposition of a more rigid structure, and the lack of flexibility in the way she did her work. But in addition, she was upset by the erosion of an old sense of community, a caring value system that seemed to support employees in their professionalism. To her, the magazine that had been a second home for many years had turned into a colder, harder place.

All of this hit Joan in a vulnerable spot; her sadness was partially triggered and precipitated by ancient feelings of losing so much of her family and her familiar surroundings at a young age.

- **Am I on shifting ground in other areas of my life at the moment?**

  Are your aging parents requiring much of your time and attention?

  Is your teenager suddenly smoking pot, failing school, or threatening to run away?

  Are you undergoing a series of medical tests and worried about the outcome?

  People who are impacted by other life-rattling events, just as work in the office demands major adjustments, might simply lack the emotional energy and calm to handle one more change. Burnout is real.

  Jack was a case in point. He had a lot on his plate. When a new supervisor with a noticeably different way of running the show entered the picture, Jack abruptly had a much harder time holding it all together.

  His life had been fairly stressful before, but he'd coped. Not only had his old boss allowed him the latitude to arrange his time according to his needs, but Jack was a regular at his gym, on most days fitting in an hour here or there for a workout on the treadmill, punching bag, and weight machines. The workouts had been a good stress buster in dealing with his family problems, but now he no longer had time for the gym. Complicating matters, Jack, always a moderate drinker, started returning to his apartment in the evenings and pouring a Scotch as soon as he walked in the door—and a few more after that. Basically, Jack was overwhelmed with anxiety that became converted to anger.

• Do I tend always to see the glass as half empty?

Temperament is part of the reactive picture. Some of us are simply and naturally more anxious or pessimistic than others, always anticipating the worst when a new regime is imposed.

• Do I have a high need for order and control in my life?

Obviously, a period of workplace change tends inevitably to reduce feelings of individual power over how the day goes.

If you would answer "yes" to any of these questions, it's highly likely that the shifting cast of characters or the changed rules, regulations, procedures, or atmosphere at work are hitting you hard. It's crucial to recognize then that your deeply felt, uncomfortable emotions just might be producing behaviors that can do you damage.

Some individuals become aggressive and hostile toward new management.

Some protect themselves by detaching from the process, a kind of cool lack of involvement.

Some are distrustful and paranoid.

Some turn into foot draggers, resisting each new adjustment.

And some might seem a bit hysterical; they overreact and are almost too eager to adapt by overcompensating.

None of this is very good. Manage those behaviors poorly, and you just *might* be out of a job.

So the next big question in an internal reality checkup is:

• How are my feelings impacting my behavior on the job?

Can you recognize any ways in which you're not handling your work too well at the moment?

Or, are others sending you clues to that effect?

Joan responded to her flood of uncomfortable emotion by becoming essentially paralyzed at her desk, failing to take necessary actions. Her anxiety, and even her response, is not unusual, considering the intensity of her internal trigger combined with a relative lack of compassionate concern from management. The new team came in, pulled a 180 in terms of established practices, and displayed not a great deal of empathy. Here's a case where an employee's story is complicated by the fact that management wasn't so benign.

She was by no means unaware of her own behaviors. "There were several times during that first month," Joan said, "when I knew I needed to ask for clarification of an assignment or some more information, and I just didn't do it. I kind of plowed on with a couple of projects, and it turned out they weren't what the editor wanted. I started to feel deeply bothered by this new person who was now reviewing my copy. I avoided her at all costs, even timing my visits to the ladies room or taking the elevator down for lunch so we wouldn't cross paths."

Joan was thinking should she stay? Should she leave? Could she complain? Was she in the wrong field entirely?

Jack wasn't entirely dysfunctional; he still got his job done. But although he wasn't making performance mistakes he was beginning to make political ones. In managing down, with his assistant and other members of his staff, his behavior was abrasive. Managing up, with the new general counsel, Jack was cool, a bit resistant. He had little to say and displayed a lack of caring. And with his peers, he began making unwise cracks about the boss, engaging in destructive gossip.

All this was anger leaking out, manifesting itself differently with the different constituencies. With his employees, the anger appeared directly; with his boss, indirectly; with his peers, in an inappropriate, politically incorrect manner.

But Jack wasn't so aware of any of this. Yes, though he was

irritated about the new boss and his style, he kept that annoyance in check—through his apparent lack of involvement. And that wasn't good.

The wake-up call came unexpectedly and took him by surprise. The HR manager let him know that one of his employees had lodged a complaint about him, giving information about abusive language and outbursts of temper. Jack was shaken and also a little scared. He was a lawyer and he understood the implications of HR involvement. Besides that, it bothered him that he'd clearly been behaving so badly that somebody complained about him. He wasn't normally a hostile guy and he didn't like being seen as one.

"That was a real alarm bell—a real consciousness-raising event. I'd been pretty oblivious to how I was acting," he said. The complaint motivated Jack to become more self-observant, and helped him realize that he had to change some behaviors if he was to survive the pressures he was under. "There were some big decisions to make for the future. Is this the time for me to jump ship, or what? I had to get my ducks in a row before I could think clearly about any of that."

For anyone feeling blindsided and overwhelmed by unwelcome change, and acting out badly as a result, the *ultimate* goal is to achieve a reasoned, reasonable choice about any subsequent actions. But here's the *immediate* goal: get a grip on yourself and behave co-operatively, so that management doesn't get you first. Avoid potential victimization by assuming responsibility and accountability, and by managing emotional responses. And jump on that very quickly.

Best next steps

First, get your act together.

When your anxiety level is very high—as it was with Joan and Jack, though they responded differently—and you realize it's getting in the way of making a clear reading and assessment of the new management and perhaps even affecting your job performance, before anything else take steps to heal yourself. If you wait for the process to run its course, just hoping that over time you'll become more resilient, better adjusted and happier, you might wait too long. So the immediate solutions should involve the following:

• Seek counseling help.

Some organizations provide internal support systems, such as a confidential employee assistance program. They might provide a few crisis counseling sessions, but if you need further support they will refer you to external mental health providers.

Support in the form of private psychotherapy, perhaps even just a few sessions with a skilled professional, can be enormously useful. Talking over worries and feelings, in a safe environment can ease the tension and clear the mind. That therapist might also recommend a referral to a psychopharmacologist for medication to quickly alleviate some symptoms. (See the box on mental health professionals on page 123.)

• Turn to your personal support system.

You need nurturing during this worrisome time.

Joan, for example, perceived herself thinking negatively, projecting bleak thoughts about the future, unwilling or unable to play the politics, and going into work with a sense of dread in the morning. "I was watching myself, like some third party, and seeing that my performance was starting to deteriorate. I began to worry that I wasn't going to survive this thing."

A smart and simple move for her is to seek the company of good friends, people who'll help get her mind off her woes. Going to the movies, having dinner out, keeping up or instigating those casual connections can help her feel supported and valued by others.

But there are various ways to shore oneself up. Some symptoms of anxiety are manifested in private behaviors that people do to cope and that common sense says aren't very healthful—overeating, drinking too much. It's a good idea to get better control. Drinking more and exercising less, for example, was a dreadful coping mechanism for Jack. In fact, increased drinking can increase anxiety, and in his case, anxiety led to greater anger. It was in his best interests to decide that whatever else was going on in his day, he had to find time to exercise, get more sleep.

• Mend fences, if necessary.

The person who responds to anxiety by angry acting-out probably needs to do a little damage control. Especially if hostile behavior or abusive language has led to official complaints, as was the case with Jack, it's crucial to demonstrate that such behavior will stop. Jack made a point of apologizing to his staff for his bursts of anger. And of course once he started to become aware of his behavior, his anger subsided and he found it easier to stick by his resolve and maintain calm with his subordinates.

• Reframe the paradigm.

By reframing the paradigm, I'm talking about consciously adopting an overall perspective—one that would be accepted by most intelligent and well-adjusted people—that explains the situation or puts it in a larger context.

Joan felt as if her world had caved in, just as she had felt when she lost her loved ones years earlier. But the truth was, no one died. Things weren't *that* bad. She might intentionally try to plant a new concept in her mind, telling herself in effect, "Well, I'm not happy about this, but it's not the end of the world. The grim reaper isn't at my door. Yes, I have to adjust to people and procedures that I'd rather not have to adjust to, and yes, it's a challenge. But I've mastered a lot in my lifetime and I can probably master this too."

As for Jack, he might need to tell himself: "This is a damn good job. I've always liked it. I do it well. The question I have to answer for myself is, is this new way I'm being asked to manage things a good fit for me, based on my personality and based on what's going on in the rest of my life? But that's a question to put off for a little while. Right now, I have to remember it's a good job and I can do good work."

Call it the power of positive thinking. Call it cognitive restructuring. It's essentially talking yourself into a more realistic assessment of what is, after all, not a life-or-death situation. And then, if possible, extend the concept and realize that though change is rampant in the corporate world, change isn't always bad. Sometimes it's good.

In order to get through this stage without causing management to perceive you as a resistant employee, or as troubled, troublesome, or incompetent, and in order to reach a position from which you're able to make a decision about staying or leaving, the first step is to get your act together. New management isn't going to read your mind and give you breathing room because of your heightened sensitivity to change and loss. So take appropriate steps to calm down. You won't necessarily have conquered every negative emotion, but you won't be acting out in self-defeating ways either.

Once your anxiety has eased, it's time to explore the external reality. Essentially, you might be stuck in the same situation, still not liking what you see. But now you can be, at least to a greater degree, an objective observer and an investigator as you go about your due diligence.

MENTAL HEALTH SERVICES

• What mental health professionals are available and what do they do?

Mental health professionals—those who have had the appropriate training and are licensed by their respective states—really consist of three types: psychologists, who hold Ph.D.'s in clinical or counseling psychology; social workers, who have master's degrees in social work; and psychiatrists, M.D.'s, some of whom practice direct mental health services such as psychotherapy and some of whom (psychopharmacologists) specialize in the utilization of medication to treat mental health problems.

Depending on your needs or wishes, you might become involved in short-term or long-term therapy. With some approaches, you can continue treatment as long as you wish; others include an agreement as to a finite amount of time. Short term is usually behavioral/cognitive therapy or goal-directed therapy, which involves changing your thought patterns or behaviors with a specific aim in mind. The longer-term model of psychodynamic therapy has as its primary focus the reduction of old conflicts and patterns, through increasing self-awareness and consciousness.

In every one of these situations, you want to begin with a clear statement of expectations and an agreement with the professional. If you're initiating psychotherapy in great distress or because you want to learn more about yourself as it relates to your work, you must expect that it might require a serious commitment and a significant amount of time.

• How can I locate a good mental health professional?

Of course, friends, family, or trusted colleagues might refer you to individual professionals. EAP might refer you. You can also

continued

contact well-regarded community mental health agencies; do an Internet search; or call professional associations, such as the American Psychological Association, your state psychological association, and social work associations.

Assembling a name or two is only the beginning. Check out the person's credentials and ask questions in an initial appointment or perhaps over the phone, especially when you're meeting someone who hasn't come personally and highly recommended from a trusted friend or colleague. The following questions are some you might ask whenever you're engaging a professional privately, whether a mental health professional, a lawyer, or a coach. Do your screening. It's perfectly appropriate to ask:

What is your educational background and your professional credentials?

Are you licensed by the state to practice?

How many years have you been practicing?

Tell me about the situations similar to mine in which you've had experience. What results or outcomes have you achieved?

What are your successes? Have you had situations in which you were not able to be helpful?

What do you like most about helping people like me?

Ask about fees, scheduling, and the professional's methodology.

Try to evaluate if this person will act as an advisor, with no bias. What you don't want in your support group from any paid consultant, be it lawyer, mental health professional, executive coach, or career coach, is someone who will judge you.

• Who pays for mental health therapy?

You! If you will be receiving therapy from a licensed professional, these services are often covered in part by insurance plans.

The external reality piece: a diagnostic questionnaire

A new management regime, occurring perhaps because company A has been sold to major conglomerate B, means new faces to deal with. But in addition to a shifting cast of characters, there might arrive a changed world order in more comprehensive terms. This might involve issues about management philosophy, culture, or values—really the integrity of the organization—and that can raise questions not only about what it will take for you to adapt, but whether you choose to.

A new supervisor might have understandable reasons for shaking up old ways of doing things. He might be receptive to suggestions on how to ease everybody over the hump. Or not.

Here's how to find out.

- **Gauge the quality of the leadership during this period of transition.**
  The following are some questions to which you might want to find answers. They apply to both the changed regime and the changed boss.

  Has the new management set clear and reasonable objectives in terms of what's expected in your job content and performance?

  Are they providing timely and direct information about shifts that are required in the way you work?

  What amount of information do they give you in a candid manner?

  Are there signs that they are attempting to honor the past? Empathizing with the fact that this time of transition might be causing everyone some anxiety?

  Do they listen and promote collaboration, or has a command/control kind of hierarchy settled in? Is there open communication? Are they responsive to your requests for information or assistance?

Does new management have a focused plan and are they consistent in following it?

What changes exactly are being imposed? Work hours? Manner of dress? More or fewer meetings?

What kind of support, if any, has been offered? (Especially when a major shift is underway, some companies will buttress employees through workshops, referrals to the employee assistance program, or individual coaching.)

Reality testing of this nature can be carried out in two ways. Some information will come to you simply by keeping your eyes and ears open over the first few months, and paying level-headed attention to the processes that are unfolding. Some information might have been obvious from day one. For example, the memos circulating in the first week told Joan that the new regime was going to be seriously concerned with cost-cutting and desk time, and some of the old pleasant perks were on the way out.

Alternately, or in addition to that kind of fact-finding investigation, peers might be able to fill you in with their impressions or experiences. Some might have a track record with the new management. Others who are going through this adjustment along with you might have found ways to help themselves along. For example, it's useful to know if the woman in the next office or down the hall received good feedback from management when she asked for it.

Remember that to gauge the quality of leadership—as you keep your eyes and ears open, as you ask questions, as you explore resources—you must come across as adaptively as possible. With your act together! With your emotions and behavior carefully managed! The new people don't know you yet. So how you present yourself can influence their responses, and you're in danger of eliciting bad ones if you appear angry, resistant, defensive, hysterical, or clearly a nervous wreck. Be careful in how you talk to coworkers. You're gathering information that you will sort through and mull over; you're not trying to stir up trouble.

Suppose that after you've conducted this stage of due diligence for a reasonable amount of time, you conclude that, by and large, new management is going about things in an appropriate manner and they're not a bad, immoral, or unfeeling bunch of people. That should at least suggest to you that maybe this change isn't so horrible. It's a situation you can accept and work within, if you decide to do so and put your mind to it. On the other hand, suppose your observations reveal that the new boss or new regime does not honor the past, demonstrates little understanding for what you and others are experiencing, fails to provide information or support, and has simply switched the rules and expected you to operate accordingly. That's not a good sign. Can you and do you want to rise to the occasion?

• Evaluate your options.

Typically, three exist: stay put and go with the flow; transfer to another position within the organization; leave, perhaps for a similar job in another company, or another kind of work entirely.

Evaluating options, of course, touches on a number of factors:

Is the field you're in a fluid one, with a lot of coming and going and jobs opening up on a regular basis?

Is your area of expertise highly valued, and thus will be much in demand elsewhere?

Do you have enough money in the bank to sustain you over a period without a salary coming in?

Have you always thought you'd like to try a completely different kind of work (and maybe the requirement to adapt now to unwanted change in your current job is the push you needed and secretly welcome)?

What degree of practical investment have you in your current job, in terms of track record, longevity, benefits, and so on?

With your emotions and acting-out behaviors well managed, with a clear analysis of the external realities of your work life, you're ready to take action.

Further best next steps

- **Conform and adapt (at least for now).**

If you've decided you won't or can't throw caution to the wind and immediately seek your fortunes elsewhere, embrace the change of new management with a positive attitude and a healthy instinct for self-preservation.

Joan and Jack, in their respective situations, reached somewhat different conclusions.

Joan looked around, asked around, and had her instincts confirmed: There were not many other places where she might jump. Because of the dearth of magazines and consolidation in the publishing business generally, jobs were scarce. In addition, the theme of cost-cutting clearly was going on elsewhere in her field. Within the staff, it was impossible to transfer to another chain of command. So this was good to know. While it's unsettling, even scary, to realize there's no easy escape, it's a piece of the picture that contributes to clear-headed solutions.

Fortunately for Joan, she had reached the conclusion that the changes she was expected to make weren't so onerous as to be impossible for her. She could still dress reasonably casually. Her immediate chains of command were not obnoxious people; they just expected greater accountability and proof of performance. Although it was a less generous environment, it wasn't an unethical one; Joan wasn't being asked to behave against her value system. There were losses—the warmth was largely gone, the sense of community was not as strong—but at the end of the day, she could make the necessary adjustments. And she was still able to do work that she enjoyed.

Jack, on the other hand, thought it was time to move on—but not just yet. Once he got his anger in control and was able to observe the new counsel's way of doing business, he realized he would continue to be expected to operate within a much more micro-managed atmosphere, with a significant loss of autonomy. This wasn't a good match for his personality and temperament, and also for his expectations as an attorney. Although it wasn't the new boss's intention, his styles of management made Jack feel somewhat devalued and distrusted.

There was no other position he could move to within the organization, so Jack made the decision to conform in the short term and act appropriately, while at the same time he would aggressively seek other employment. Over the longer term, he knew he would continue to need more flexibility in order to handle his personal life, which would remain complicated even after his divorce was resolved. He began quietly exploring opportunities in law firms and investigating what possibilities existed for setting up his own practice.

- **Compensate elsewhere for the sense of loss that unwanted change has produced.**

    Especially if going to work once was like again joining one's second family, a home away from home, adapting to a changed environment also means resolving to find externally some of those good feelings. Maybe that will include deciding to stop giving 110 percent to the job; maybe 95 percent will take care of it just fine. And then, with determination and a bit more energy, join a book club, volunteer in a soup kitchen, or go to the museum.

    Change can bring a sense of loss. It can also open new doors.

6

NEW TECHNOLOGY

HOW TO FACE UP TO FEARS (AND BITE A NECESSARY BULLET)

Perhaps you have recently had to face an imposed change to your office life something like the following:

An advanced computer operating system has been installed and you will be expected henceforth to communicate and present data within a network, which comes with complicated-sounding rules.

You've assumed a new position that will require you to make PowerPoint presentations, something you haven't done before.

Teleconferencing and telecommuting are becoming established aspects of your place of business, and new gadgets have arrived in your office.

You have some catching up to do. How will you handle that?

Here's my first suggestion: Accept it.

Technology changes are inundating all levels and aspects of

our lives. In particular, new technology is flooding the workplace. Yes, much has happened over the past 20 or so years; we have all been required to apply ourselves to fresh challenges. But still more is on the horizon. At this moment in time, anyone in corporate America who's unaware that he or she is inescapably engaged in a continual skill-building process is in trouble. As an employee, you must be a lifelong learner, because technology advances are inevitable and on-going. You cannot escape them. This doesn't mean you'll embrace them with joy and enthusiasm.

It's probably accurate to say that most of us, regardless of individual blind spots, will respond to imposed technology changes with some dismay. The feeling is, "Oh brother, here's just one more thing I have to do, as if I'm not busy and pressured enough already." For some, however, the requirement to master additional skills can stir up powerful anxieties. And dreading the advance of technology can easily trigger behaviors that potentially derail you, cause you to be less successful, or even threaten your job.

In this chapter, we look at:

- Adapting to new technology—and how employee Roxanne coped

New technology might be imposed by your bosses for cost-cutting or other organizational reasons. Or, as the specialty you're in continues to evolve, mastering new procedures is necessary if you are to remain in the forefront of your field. In either case, the personal issues associated with this form of change do not typically involve feelings of sadness and loss, as tends to be true when facing the imposition of new management. We're exploring here not so much underlying psychology (although that's part of the picture), but rather how and why you might have a hard time learning something new. And that might have to do with the fear of failure—or in some individuals, conversely, the fear of success.

Roxanne's story: what happened to her one day on the job

Roxanne, 45, was a well-regarded associate in a midlevel advertising company that handled accounts in the personal and home products areas. She was doing work she loved and was good at it.

"I'm great with focus groups," she said, "great with overall concepts. I'm an idea person. I spark off people; I come up with my best stuff by bouncing off others." In the presentation of her ideas on the job, she'd always been able to wing it without any fancy technology. Roxanne had been in advertising for 20 years, and hoped to go on for another 20. Her current job suited her to a tee: She could be around other creative types, have plenty of time at home with her husband and their two teenagers, and jot down sales pitches in the middle of the night if she wanted.

Her bosses had no complaints with Roxanne's work, but they recently had begun exploring ways to modernize and streamline several company operations. In a consolidation move, it was decided that Roxanne would take on some new responsibilities, one of which required budgeting. They also wanted to get information out more quickly along the chain of command, and had come up with some processes for that.

One morning Roxanne found on her desk a packet of information describing software that would shortly be installed on her computer and that she would be expected to use in the future. A note attached from the manager called this an exciting development that he believed would facilitate the way Roxanne worked. She'd still be the individual contributor she had been, still the ideas person, but she'd now add some skills in preparing spreadsheets, using scanners, and on-line communication. She would be provided with appropriate training by the company.

She detested the whole idea.

Roxanne first explained her resistance as a reasonable reaction to what she believed was an unproductive switch being foisted on her. "I am a 100 percent creative type," she said. "I can do e-mailing, but that's about it. So why put me into this dry, dull, mechanical stuff. It's counterintuitive."

Actually, she was petrified at the thought of having to work within this technology. More than that: she was sure she'd never be able to manage it. That was her blind spot. "I'm the classic techno-phobe. My kids bought me a fancy cell phone for my birthday, and so far all I do on it is press 'talk.' Anyway, at this stage of the game, it's just not so easy to figure out a whole new way of running my job."

Technophobes do exist. We all know someone—or maybe we *are* that "someone"—who views technology as an alien and vaguely threatening force.

It's also true that somewhat older people, accustomed to estab-lished work patterns, might have anxious and pessimistic attitudes about having to become full-fledged members of the technological age. Young employees tend to be more comfortable, exposed to it as they have been from childhood. If you're a 22-year-old just starting your first after-college job, the computer is right there on your desk from day one, as familiar and unscary as a telephone.

But in addition:

Some people, young or old, are simply not fast learners. Pick-ing up on new technology will not be a natural strength, skill base, or competency.

Others aren't particularly motivated to explore advanced pro-cedures. These folks prefer the status quo; by temperament, they're inclined to avoid any change in their way of working.

Still others were not great students. They struggled in school, perhaps experiencing special difficulties in math or the more con-crete kinds of study.

And of course, if new technology arrives just as other life changes need to be dealt with—a divorce, a move, a medical crisis, even a kitchen renovation—that person can be too distracted or stressed to address additional workplace demands in a calm and confident manner.

Any of these factors might be making you especially vulnerable to anxiety or distaste in the face of imposed changing technology. However, if you don't get a grip on those emotions, they can disrupt the learning process even if your company provides a good deal of support and even if you're basically a capable individual. Manage your feelings or you might land yourself in a self-fulfilling prophecy: You are convinced you'll mess up and so you do.

What does your internal reality reveal?

The internal reality piece: a diagnostic questionnaire

When adapting to new technology on the job can't be avoided, and when the need to do so is extremely frightening, people respond in various ways. You may find yourself foot-dragging—not signing up for the training session, or in other ways directly or indirectly stubbornly resisting any real show of cooperation. Or, you make a stab at taking in the new information, but discover you have difficulty retaining it; you're making lots of mistakes. Or, you become somewhat paralyzed, so overwhelmed that you're not even trying to acquire the necessary skills.

Not good.

So here are some questions to help you explore what's going on inside and what might be behind those responses:

- **What am I afraid of?**

Typically and most simply, one views new technology as complicated, difficult, a foreign language, and off-putting in the extreme. Consequently, one harbors the feeling: "I won't be able to do this; I'm going to look dumb." And then: "What happens to me when I can't do this?"

That's fear of failure.

However, there is another and opposite dynamic that may come into play and that manifests in a similar tendency to resist learning new skills: fear of success. This trickier and essentially unconscious emotion is especially common in first-generation employees who have reached management levels and whose accomplishments have far exceeded those of their parents. Fear of success may be triggered by an unwitting reluctance to surpass mom and dad even further in terms of their achievements, because to do so would mean distancing yet again from family and roots. And so to avoid those uncomfortable feelings, this employee unconsciously resists living up to his potential.

For most of us, it's fear of failure that holds us back.

Nobody wants to be found inadequate for the job, nobody wants to look dumb, but fear of failure intensifies under certain circumstances.

Is there a risk that if you don't adapt, you'll be terminated? If it's very clear that the new technology is not just a secondary support, but in fact is essential to success on your job, maybe even to keeping it, that's an added pressure.

Do you have to teach somebody else what you're just learning? If you are managing people, not only is the technology change imposed on *you*, but on them as well. And you'll be responsible for helping others adjust to something you're just trying to get a grip on yourself. You'll have to be both student and teacher.

All this stirs up anxiety. An internal reality exploration, then, continues:

- **What makes me convinced I'm never going to be able to learn this new technology?**

  Think back.

  Was school a largely supportive or hideously unpleasant learning environment?

If teachers in your past—or maybe your parents—tended to be unhelpful, disapproving, disappointed, or critical when you were unable quickly to grasp a subject that was difficult for you, memories of those ancient stressful times may be triggering current anxieties. Faced with having to learn new tricks on the job, you can feel as if you're right back in those bad old days, when your efforts to do well and please your elders weren't too successful. So you may need to remind yourself that this isn't school, you are an adult, and you're going to be quite capable of recognizing when you need help and asking for it.

Are you considered—perhaps fondly—the family klutz? Are you used to having everyone else assume mechanical day-to-day tasks?

Roxanne, for example, said her ineptitude in certain areas was a kind of joke in her house. "One of my kids said the other day, 'Okay, here's one for you, how long does it take Mom to change a lightbulb? Answer: As long as it takes Dad to get in from the other room and do it for her.' Ha, ha. But it's true, my husband and the kids are very handy and basically fearless about gadgets, and they take care of anything having to do with the computers, the cable boxes, the VCR, the DVD, all that stuff—anything with wires."

There's nothing inherently wrong with letting other willing hands and minds deal with matters that cause you to struggle, but a history of doing so might be reinforcing the conviction that you're just lousy at anything vaguely technical and you always will be. Or, maybe that history has convinced you there's always a way out, someone else will step in to pick up the slack, and so there's no real need to apply yourself. These are mental attitudes you will do well to overcome.

Do you peg yourself a "creative type," someone who's "all about ideas"? It may be true that mastering cold technology is not a natural competency for you. That doesn't mean, however, that it's beyond your capabilities. Your creative self-identity needn't be threatened or under-mined by working up skills in different areas.

- **In the past, *when* was I successful at learning something new and *how* did I do it?**

Once again, cast back and this time recall previous triumphs, even if they were small ones. We all have had at least one or two. How did you learn to drive a car? How did you get a passing grade in chemistry, once you realized you had no aptitude or love for science? How did you figure out how to e-mail, or record a message on your answering machine?

These reflections tell you something about your style of learn-ing, or the way you typically are most successful at acquiring com-petency in an area. For example:

Did you learn and retain information best by reading a manual, and poring over it again and again if necessary? What works for you is to go at the task on your own, aiming all your attention on the writ-ten page without distraction and for as long as it takes.

On the other hand, many people cannot assimilate information by reading a set of instructions. Perhaps you're one of them. You've always needed a hands-on someone to sit next to you and show you, saying: Press this button, press that button, now do this, now do that.

Have you had prior good luck in a group situation? When your chemistry grades were looking dismal, you organized an informal study group with a couple of friends and worked at problems to-gether? The company of others, all of you starting from the same place and shooting for the same goal, gave you a boost and helped you focus.

Review how you have succeeded in the past when you were challenged by having to learn something new. That pattern of suc-cess is probably what you need to reconstruct here.

This kind of self-analysis can go a long way toward transforming the amorphous, free-floating anxiety you experience when staring at the new software or gadget on the job, into an understandable, manageable, maybe even interesting challenge.

Tame the tiger. Then look at what's going on outside you.

The external reality piece: a diagnostic questionnaire

Due diligence involves exploring what you're expected to do and when, and how much help you're going to get along the way. So first consider:

- **Do I really have to do this?**

  Maybe you *can* get out of it.

  Without coming across as a terrified, resistant foot dragger or a sulky child, find out if it is in fact possible to delegate these new tasks to someone else. That's not going to work in every situation, of course, but sometimes an added technological demand can be handled by an assistant or a part-time temp. Inquire amiably if such might be the case in your office. If you're met with a clear "no" or a stony look—your boss is obviously wondering now if you have the right stuff at all—let the matter drop. You don't want to risk your job or appear too much as one stuck in the Stone Age.

  In addition, look around some more. Call a colleague or two in other similar firms, if you have them. Are the new skills becoming the industry standard and therefore expected of any company you might move to? If so, you don't have much of an out.

- **Okay, if I really have to do this, how much time will I be allowed to bring myself up to speed?**

  This should be one of your first questions as management or your supervisor describes to you the changed requirements.

  What will be the expectations and measurements for performance in the new technology?

What will be the time frame between the learning period and actually performing on the job, when fouling up will have an impact on business? If it seems unrealistic—you'll be given a week to master things and then the old procedure will be immediately defunct— there's nothing wrong with suggesting, again amiably, that a more extended learning period might be required, and could that please be arranged.

- **Am I on my own or is the company prepared to help me?**

If you have sympathetic management that realizes this change is a tough one for its employees, it can make all the difference between success and failure—or if not outright failure, the difference between a relatively stress-free period of retraining or a stomach-acid-producing stretch of misery.

Sympathetic management is one that provides educational or training help, a reasonable time frame, and encouragement and appreciation of the adjustments that have to be made. Unsympathetic management is one that throws a lot of new and different stuff at you at once, and then leaves you essentially on your own to meet a quick learning curve. The more you're left unaided to sink or swim, the more pressure you're likely to have regardless of your vulnerabilities. Even a young employee with decent tech confidence in an organization that unfairly refuses to provide support and time may be more stressed than the shakier individual within a sympathetic one.

Some organizations establish a reward system that places incentives to learn new technology. That, too, can certainly help you overcome your resistance.

If your organization clearly is going to be helpful, count your blessings and resolve to make the best of the support you'll be offered. If no provision has been made for training, and you know you're going to need it, you have two options. Ask your manager if someone on the staff with the necessary expertise can be assigned to walk you through the initial stages of adapting to your new responsibilities. Or, make it clear that you will require some training; it won't take too long; you'll find an appropriate outside source for that, and you hope you will be reimbursed for the cost. That may or may not work, but it's worth a try.

Best next steps

• Talk yourself into a better frame of mind.

As always, a positive outlook eases the strain, and a positive outlook is something you can actively pursue, all on your own. Tell yourself: "Get a grip. Don't panic. This new technology is not a terrible thing that's out to get me; it's simply one aspect of my being a working member of society at this time. This is not school. I don't have to focus on failing or not failing, just on learning and adapting. Other people have done it. I can do it too."

Go for confidence building. Reassure yourself it's not going to be as bad as you think. And keep on reassuring yourself as you wade into the learning process.

• Fight for the kind of training that works for you.

Not all technicians, even those who are hired to train, are skilled teachers. Some are fairly awful, in fact—good at the expertise and dreadful at conveying it to others. They're technicians, not tutors. That's when you can become intimidated and anxious all over again, to the point of paralysis: The "expert" has just explained a procedure to you, you have no idea what he's talking about, you assume you're not getting it because you simply are a dolt, and you say nothing. Your confidence withers, and the old message in your head returns: "I knew I'd never be able to do this."

Roxanne, for example, was provided by her company with a computer technician who would train her in the new programs. He had one hour each morning to devote to her, and then he moved on to others in the organization. After the first two sessions, Roxanne was as befuddled as ever. "Craig, that's his name, is a perfectly cheerful fellow. He comes in, sits down in my chair in front of the computer, and rattles off a list of things I should be doing, as he does them himself—'Open this window, hit this command, highlight that, now you want to click on this, now you want to scroll down that.' All this time I'm standing behind him, so I'm not at an angle where I can even see that well what's going on. And my brain isn't keeping up with what he's saying. I don't know all these technical terms, but I don't want to stop him to ask what something means, because he's on to the next step."

Remember that your technical support person is working for you, and you may need to teach him how to teach you. Many trainers have little appreciation or awareness of different learning styles. Make sure you get what you need.

So Roxanne may have to tell Craig: "Look, I'm not following you. I need to be more hands-on here, so I'm going to sit in front of the computer and you sit over there and talk me slowly through the steps. That way I'll have more of a feel for the process."

If you learn best from instruction manuals, have your support person go over the pages with you as you ask questions and make notes.

Whether help is coming one-on-one or in a group session, don't be afraid to stop the action and ask for clarification or repetition. Don't be afraid to look a little slow.

Even if the organization offers training courses, it's often a good idea to pay out of your pocket for an external consultant who's an expert in the area. You'll have more confidence that you can master the new learning. In addition, depending on your situation and office atmosphere, you may wish to keep a lid on your vulnerabilities in the company-provided training program, and kind of hit the deck running with some private tutoring under your belt.

• **Search out a model of inspiration.**

Talk to a friend or coworker who's gone successfully through a similar learning process. Absorb reassurance from that individual.

"One of the designers was also starting to work with new programs," Roxanne said, "and he seemed to just magically gravitate to it. Actually, within a week he was loving the whole thing and very jazzed about how the job was changing. I realized that if he likes it and can do it, it must mean it's okay."

When you're in the midst of learning something new, different, and difficult, it's hard to believe you will ever come to actually enjoy what you're doing. You just may, however. And you won't be the first employee who started out kicking and struggling, only to realize once over the initial hump that the new technology was pretty neat, and fun, and exciting.

• **If you suspect fear of success is holding you back, talk that over with a professional.**

Earlier, I mentioned that resistance to mastering a new skill or technology is sometimes caused by an unrecognized wish not to do better in life than one's parents. That's separating from family and roots; that's painful. Those unconscious feelings are so strong and pervasive that they're difficult to overcome through personal determination, a good mental attitude, or "willpower." In such situations, seeking a consultation with a mental health professional can be a saving grace. (See the information on mental health professionals on page 123.)

In this chapter, we've focused on the employee within a corporate structure. But fear of technology isn't a trigger for corporate workers only. Entrepreneurs and consultants who provide their services to organizations also get hit with the anxieties that can come with having to undo old patterns of skills and learn new ones.

PART 3

SURVIVING SHADES OF GRAY

A FEW FIRST THOUGHTS

The following three chapters—*The Highly Politicized Office, Confused Directives,* and *Mission Impossible*—share some common themes. Each describes work environments colored in shades of gray.

You're not quite sure what's going on, or where and how to put your finger on the unease you are feeling, or if you're just not "getting" it while you think everyone else is. Shades of gray can trigger not only uncomfortable emotions, but behaviors on the job by which you can easily shoot yourself in the foot if you're not careful.

7

THE HIGHLY POLITICIZED OFFICE

HOW TO KNOW WHEN CURRYING FAVOR MIGHT BE MORE IMPORTANT THAN PROVING YOUR MERIT

Once upon a time, corporate America was run largely as a meritocracy. Salary, praise, advancement, and status, all were based primarily, or sometimes exclusively, on how well you carried out your tasks. That picture has changed.

Success in the office today, getting ahead on the job, often has a great deal to do with being perceived as a comfortable piece of the organizational puzzle, whatever form that takes—perceived as an insider, basically. If you fit within the puzzle, you're considered important to the company. You're more successful. Especially at higher levels, political acumen—the ability to establish valued interpersonal connections—might be rewarded as much as or more than the achievement of job goals.

But what does "playing politics" in the office mean? Is it uniformly a negative and nasty business, in which only the shrewdest and wiliest employees win? If you're no good at cozying up to the right people, are you out of luck?

There are two sides to the story, and it is both impossible and unhelpful to make the value judgment that a highly politicized office is per se an awful place to work. If the truly crafty employees who use any expediencies to get ahead, trampling on their peers in the process, are continually advanced through the organization, then that's a toxic politicized environment. If the guy who makes a point of playing golf on the weekends with the senior manager gets a fatter bonus than the guy who does the same amount of quality work but doesn't play golf, that might be considered unfair.

On the other hand, the relatively recent appreciation of emotional intelligence—the term coined by Daniel Goleman in his book of that name—is one of the positive aspects of the politicized office, as companies are becoming more sensitive to the fact that other criteria besides task achievement count towards business success. Often, people who demonstrate empathy and consensus building, who get along well with others and are cooperative, are the ones who rise, even if they're not the strongest in technical expertise. And it might be, in fact, that this tendency is a sign of growth in terms of organizational wisdom.

What matters, of course, is whether *you* have the behavioral strengths, and the determination and stamina, to accommodate the often subtle requirements of office politics. Some people will have a harder time of it than others. In this chapter, we look at three types of individuals who might especially struggle. We consider:

- Office politics—and how Shelley, the good student, coped
- Office politics—and how Nathan, the independent, coped
- Office politics—and how Peter, the moralist, coped

The scenarios that follow sketch out some of the pitfalls and strategies involved in surviving in a politicized environment, and you might find bits and pieces of yourself in each. Maybe you're something of the good student, the independent, the moralist, all in one package. How good are you at playing politics? Do you want to?

Shelley's story: what happened to her one day on the job

After four years of outstanding performance, Shelley, 28, had no doubts she'd achieve her next career goal shortly. Employed by a national hotel and resorts chain with facilities in every city across the country, she started out as a local service representative responsible for handling telephone hotline complaints or suggestions from customers. Shelley had worked her way up to senior service rep, and then was promoted to manager level. In that job, she also assumed responsibilities for aspects of online marketing for the chain. For the past six months Shelley had had her eye on the next step, Mid-Atlantic regional manager.

She believed she was highly qualified for the job. "No one can say I haven't done outstanding work here," Shelley said. "Excellent customer ratings reports. People have actually written to the company to say how helpful I was. I've had commendations from the organization in each of the last three years, raises. With my promotion, I was made supervisor of three of the local reps and I work well with them. I've delivered real results for this place."

With this undeniably solid track record in her favor, Shelley was astounded and crushed when Helen, another employee at her level, was awarded the regional manager's spot. Both women had the same boss, a vice president Shelley didn't see or talk to very often. "His office is in headquarters, which I don't have any reason to go to, and he's not a particularly hands-on person. He didn't have to be. I have a once a year meeting with him to go over my evaluations; he's always been satisfied."

Being passed over for the promotion hit her hard. Shelley began to get depressed, feeling the rules had changed on her.

Shelley had kept her head down, focused on her tasks, and been rewarded for her achievements with gold stars, added responsibilities, and salary increases. This is not at all unusual in the early stages of a corporate career, which are usually meritocracy based. Even in a highly political work environment, diligence, ability to follow through, conscientiousness, all these propel many achievers into excellent entry level positions in which they shine. It's a lot like school, really, where academic success is about personal effort—you work hard, you get a good grade. In corporate life, while you're still lower on the food chain, that might be all that matters. Shelley fit the good student syndrome to a tee.

The trouble with the meritocracy/school model is that it doesn't prepare an employee for the interpersonal/political aspect of office behavior at a higher level. At some point during a career—the point Shelley had probably reached, involving a jump to a more senior position—other traits, styles, and competencies usually begin to weigh more heavily towards success: daring, risk taking, self-promoting, the ability to manage up, relationship building.

Though I've made an effort throughout this book to remain gender neutral—since my professional coaching with men and women has so often been similar in terms of their reactions to trigger situations—it's in this area that differences do reveal themselves more acutely. In my experience, women tend to have a harder time than men shifting from the meritocratic to the political requirements of the workplace, or practicing a useful combination of the two as they go about their daily business. Much research has pointed out that girls outperform boys from kindergarten to graduate school, because good student behavior is recognized. But in the corporate world, when those other traits and styles come into account, many women have difficulty picking up strategies that seem to come more naturally to many men.

Shelley had to think through some of her preconceptions about what the job called for—and why, just possibly, her proven track record apparently wasn't enough to get her the promotion.

The internal reality piece: a diagnostic questionnaire

If you pride yourself on being a worker bee who keeps her eye on the job, you value your performance successes, as you should. If despite your performance successes you seem stuck on a rung of the career ladder—*and* you are starting to suspect there's something you should be doing that you're not—ask:

• How am I measuring my success on the job?

Would you point exclusively to results-oriented, quantifiable proof that you are doing good work? It's all right there on the page, the numbers or other measures that speak to your competence?

If you can't see beyond those indicators, maybe it's time to broaden your perspective and acknowledge to yourself a degree of tunnel vision that might be impeding your progress.

• Is my self-esteem tied directly to achievements?

Thinking back, was getting top grades in school the only goal? Making all A's not only made you happy, it meant you were a worthwhile person?

This habit of connecting success and self-esteem to the need to achieve often has its origins in childhood or student days—and it's a habit that's not always so applicable in the adult world of work.

• Do I know how to incorporate better people skills into my job performance?

Or, we might say, do you have a sense of what playing politics is all about? It's possible that you absorbed messages on that score long ago, messages that have left you a bit clueless.

For example, if you lived with parents who persistently conveyed the belief that currying favor in order to get ahead was a cheesy or unnecessary thing to do, you probably grew up with one of two kinds of issues—either ineptitude, or a lack of skills, or antipathy, the dislike of anything remotely political. You shouldn't have to bring an apple to the teacher if your grades were good, was the general idea—and in fact doing so would be a bit dishonest or beneath you. Maybe these parents refused to "play the game" in their own professional or social lives; maybe that worked out well or, on the other hand, they suffered because of it, and so found much righteous justification for their opinions.

As always, the goal of an internal reality investigation is to understand your feelings, attempt to analyze what might be prompting them, and lessen their impact on your behavior. Depending on your blind spot and personality, you might become frustrated, angry, depressed, or sad if you seem to be not fitting into the organizational puzzle and you're watching others meet that challenge effortlessly. Try not to let those emotions derail you at work.

Then decide what you can do about it all.

The external reality piece: a diagnostic questionnaire

• Who's getting ahead in this organization and why?

Can you discern what kinds of behaviors are rewarded, or perhaps which are frowned on?

Can you pick up useful clues just by observation of individuals' styles, personality traits, and manners?

Or, maybe the question is, who are the popular people and what are they doing that makes them popular?

Do they make a point of reaching out to others? Linger a little after work hours to fraternize with coworkers, instead of heading for the door? Linger a little after a meeting to chat with the boss? Sign on for the company softball team? Do they dress well?

If you conclude that "office politics" in your office is relatively benign, nothing too cutthroat or back-stabbing is going on, you have further confirmation that you might be out of the loop because of your own shortcomings or blind spots.

In conducting her due diligence, Shelley learned some interesting facts, including from Helen, the coworker who got the coveted promotion. Although the two had been after the same position, she and Helen were friendly and liked each other, and once Shelley moved past her initial disappointment and depression, she took Helen out to lunch. They talked. "She told me she often dropped in at the boss's office over the past couple of years, just to say 'hi,' " Shelley said, "because he liked that kind of personal contact. He'd take a break; they'd go down to the cafeteria for coffee. A couple of times they had lunch and talked about the business."

This was eye-opening news to Shelley. While she had been sticking to the work at hand, confident in her good performance output, Helen, it seemed, had been sensitive to the fact that their boss valued being managed in a social way. Shelley hadn't developed any interpersonal relationship with the boss; he was there simply to go over her once-a-year evaluations.

Shelly added: "I just happened to read an article that said, 'Dress for the next job you want to have,' and it hit me, wow! That's certainly something Helen did. And I didn't." In Shelley's first job at the organization, she had worn jeans and sweaters, "always clean and neat looking, and that was okay. When I got to manager level, I dressed up a little more, but still very casual, I like to be comfortable." Unlike her coworker, Shelley didn't start dressing like a regional manager. "You don't have to look like you're working for a Wall Street firm around here," Shelley said, "but I can see that the upper-level people do have a kind of sophisticated image. And as a regional manager, you're expected to do some traveling; you go to some corporate dinners and functions. Maybe I didn't look like I'd be prepared for that."

She thought it was time to improve her act.

Best next steps

• Pay greater attention to visual impressions.

Call it superficial, call it insulting. Then try to adapt to what seem to be generally admired appearances around the office. In all likelihood, management has not been sending out edicts about appropriate modes of dress. But if your external reality check indicated that two well-favored employees who are clearly on the fast track always show up in tailored linen suits and silk blouses and tasteful jewelry, maybe that's a look you should emulate—especially if you've been wearing slacks and sweaters forever. If a highly valued coworker leaves her office neat and cleared at the end of the day and always has fresh flowers and a bowl of candy on her desk, there's a clue for you.

In some organizations, visual impressions count for a lot.

• Be a little pushy.

Not *too* pushy. But when interpersonal connections are clearly contributing to getting ahead, it's in your best interests to do what needs to be done to nurture relationships. That might mean observing and paying attention to the organization leaders, the decision makers, and getting to know them. Find ways of being helpful. If you learn your senior manager has a keen interest in a certain corporate client, let's say, and you have knowledge in that area, you might want to send the manager an e-mail and provide him further information. You look as if you are adding value to the corporation. If you know a senior executive is on the board of a particular community group, perhaps you will want to let her know that you think highly of that organization and are volunteering your time there.

If management is proud of the company softball team, join the softball team.

• Practice the art of detached engagement.

Shelley had come to accept that delivering "real results" wasn't always more important than making the right connections. Looking ahead, she wasn't sure when another promotion possibility would arise, but she became determined to manage her bosses better from then on. She'd make some of those cosmetic changes, the nicer wardrobe. And, she said, "I'm not going to take this so personally. It's sort of like I've figured out a script I should follow, and I can do that."

That's wise. That's the art of detached engagement: Make the best of the situation, control the impact on your self-esteem by separating your ego, continue to perform, and do what's necessary to fit in.

So here's one way to decide you'll survive in a politicized office. You need not *value* these behaviors, you can believe they're not highly admirable or they're a little silly. At the same time, you can convince yourself that you can and should adapt, and you will not take it all to heart so much. "Playing politics" is an apt phrase. This is a bit of a game, a lot like Monopoly. It's worth your while to get in the game.

Nathan's story: what happened to him one day on the job

Six months into a new job with a technical communications firm, Nathan, 30, was frustrated to the point of despair. He actually was doing essentially the same work as before, but he was unable to do it in the same old way. That was driving him nuts.

He'd worked for several years on a medical newsletter with a small mailing list among physicians, hospitals, and health care workers. "There were just three of us," Nathan said, "Really two of us—my boss, who started and funded the newsletter, and me. Then we had a third person, usually on a temp basis, who took care of some of the mechanics." He greatly admired his boss, an older man with an academic background. What Nathan especially liked was the ease with which he could do his own work, which involved researching, interviewing, and writing most of the reports that made up the newsletter. "John, my boss, and I were on the same wavelength, and he trusted my instincts completely about the areas we should cover."

Then the boss decided it was time to retire and to accept a buyout offer from a large corporation that marketed a variety of materials in the medical, health, library, and technology fields. Nathan went with the new company, excited about possibilities he foresaw. "There would be more financing available; we could put out a bigger and better-looking publication." Disillusionment set in before long.

"My little newsletter is now part of a division in which a bunch of disparate products are lumped under the same umbrella," Nathan said, "The man who's head of this unit is constantly having the staff get together to talk about marketing and other factors. 'Synergy,' that's his favorite word. Everybody seems to like him. What I see is that he's not particularly original, and there's a lot of compromising. More than once, I've had to go along with some decision because it satisfied the average." Nathan was also now asked to solicit the input of others in the division about trends he wanted to pursue.

He described himself as in a no-win situation. "I'm stuck between a rock and a hard place. Leaving doesn't make any sense, financially or otherwise. My kind of experience is hard to translate. But there's a price I'm paying for working this way. Loss of independence, acceptance of less than the highest standards. In that sense, it's a step down from how I used to work."

Conditioned by a highly meritocratic environment in which

he was judged solely on his intelligence and task performance, Nathan essentially thought that was the way the world went. In addition, he was accustomed to working independently, answering to no one except the boss who knew and supported his strengths. Along came an organization that encouraged teamwork, that required sharing of ideas and promoted the goal of synergy, and Nathan was blindsided.

Was he stuck between a rock and a hard place?

The internal reality piece: a diagnostic questionnaire

- **Do I really believe consensus building is bad for the business, or is it just bad for me?**

  Here's another way of thinking about that issue:

  Are you so unhappy with the socializing or interpersonal aspect of the job that you've convinced yourself socializing can't possibly be productive? That's not what work is all about?

  In a politicized office that values relationship building and teamwork, the employees who fit the organizational puzzle most easily tend to be those who have no problem offering opinions and listening to the opinions of others, all with an open mind and a generous outlook. Or, the ones who fit in are the extroverts, the natural schmoozers who thrive and become energized in the give-and-take of a lively work environment. If you are not one of those, are you dismissing the group approach out of hand?

- **Does it make me feel rejected, ignored, or belittled to be just one among several in an office work situation?**

  Do you have to be the star? Did you always have to be?

  In thinking through his internal reality, Nathan made this observation. "I'm an only child and the proverbial apple of my parents' eyes, and all through childhood they led me to understand that I was superior to other kids. They basically told me in various ways that I could do better than anybody. I love them for that, my personal cheering squad, and of course soon enough I discovered there were other superior kids in the world too." But throughout school he always liked "to shine alone, have the spotlight. Even the sports I gravitated to weren't the team variety."

The lifelong introvert or the "star" won't change his colors overnight, but it helps to get clear in your own mind how much of your annoyance, resentment, discomfort, anger, or whatever you are feeling is generated by those personal blind spots.

The external reality piece: a diagnostic questionnaire

- **Am I being treated fairly? Am I listened to?**

  If there is a great deal of psychological pushing and shoving going on among the team members, one-upping to gain dominance, that's obviously not so pleasant and you might be in the environment we explore in Peter's story, coming up next. On the other hand, if teamwork runs smoothly—individuals are met with courtesy, equal time, and mutual respect—assume you should be able to find your place in the system.

- **Is the teamwork atmosphere bringing down the quality of the output?**

  Are things so bad? Is the work suffering because of a push for consensus?

  Once you've contained your emotional responses, it should not be too difficult to analyze what's going on. Is the need to compromise, to accept "less than the highest standards" as you perceive them, damaging? Maybe satisfying the average turns out to be not so deleterious to the business in the long run.

Best next steps

- **Try—hard—to become more of a team player.**

  Practice the fine art of compromise.

  Nathan, for example, had to modify some of his old ways of going about his work. Instead of writing a report and sending it through, perhaps he needed first to solicit ideas from the others in his division, make the final product more of a collective effort. Maybe he had consciously to accept an extended time span in which to achieve his technical goals; it was going to take longer to resolve projects and bring them to fruition because of consensus-oriented procedures in his office.

  You do not have to turn yourself into a hail fellow well met individual to become a better team player. You do, probably, have to recognize and seize small, day-to-day opportunities to engage coworkers with whom you share joint goals.

  This is not an easy adjustment. If all along you've built your notion of success around being an outstanding independent contributor, focused on task results, you'll now have to work on the personality factors and preferences and habits that have served you well in the past. Tinker with them in order to bring some of your behaviors more in line with company politics. More than that, in fact: You'll be wise to adjust your broader understanding—what I call reframing the paradigm. In other words:

- **Believe in a different model of success.**

  When a politicized environment emphasizes teamwork, that's not necessarily unfortunate. It might be a significant and valuable way of implementing a business strategy. It might be what works best for everyone in the long run. So the coping process—how you survive—is more than just adapting certain behaviors to fit the rules; ideally, it involves *believing* that the rules are appropriate and all to the good.

If Nathan decides to stick it out and go along on the job, but harbors a persistently negative attitude about what he perceives to be useless politics, he's likely eventually to sabotage himself in some way. In order to succeed in his changed environment, he has to believe, not just act as if, the criteria for success are right for the business.

Peter's story: what happened to him one day on the job

Peter, 31, was an accountant in the staff department of a large food products firm. Three years after he had taken the job, a raft of organizational changes brought in a new management team; it wasn't long before those changes at the top began to produce noticeable shifts at Peter's level. The CEO had swiftly installed his hand-picked primary managers, including a CFO who became Peter's boss. In the new culture, it was clear to everyone that a largely meritocratic environment had become a more politicized one. Peter's new supervisor, the CFO, at once struck Peter as a rather narcissistic individual who surrounded himself with "yes men."

Peter, to his satisfaction, had been evaluated on the basis of his expertise. He, too, was a task-focused worker. Actually, he had been fortunate under the previous regime. Employees who hold staff or professional jobs in a large organization—that is, who work in the nonrevenue-producing, support areas such as human resources, legal, and financial departments—often are greatly impacted by politics. These individuals, whose performance cannot always be measured quantitatively, tend to be judged often by their relationship skills—frankly, whether people like you or not.

Peter wasn't aware of that reality, either in the old days or currently. "I've always been a straightforward, bottom line guy," he said. "I didn't have to think about the proper way to approach the boss, the proper way to present things. All that's gone out the window." Not only did he feel he could no longer communicate in the old style; he was coming to believe that his opinions were undervalued because of his "bottom line" mentality. "We work in numbers here, there's a clear right and a clear wrong. But you go into a meeting now, and everybody's running for Mr. and Ms. Popularity. The sucking-up that goes on is enough to turn your stomach."

Peter had planted his flag in the sand, determined not to be caught up in the popularity contests and sticking to his convictions that high professional standards and excellent performance should be sufficient. Increasingly, however, he was feeling marginalized. He also believed that two of the most egregious "yes men" were getting special attentions. "There is so much jockeying for position, so much jollying up going on," Peter said, "and it really is all about currying favor with this guy who likes getting his ego stroked."

All this was taking a physical toll. In fact, perhaps from sitting through those meetings he found so stomach turning, he began developing actual gastrointestinal problems, and high blood pressure as well. His comfort level in the office was reaching an all-time low.

Could he survive in his politicized environment?

The internal reality piece: a diagnostic questionnaire

- **Do I feel like a fake when I try to be a people-pleaser?**

    Does it stick in your craw to make appreciative noises to a boss or management, when you perceive that's the kind of behavior that goes over well?

    Take a temperature reading of the level of your distaste. If it's way up there, you're in for a bumpy ride.

- **Do I have strong moral objections to what I see going on here?**

    What's going on is not illegal or immoral. Nevertheless, do you still believe the office politics you're observing is wrong? How *deeply* do you believe it to be wrong? This is a bit of self-analysis that gets to the heart of what makes you tick—and that at the end of the day might be the determining factor in whether or not you survive your tricky workplace situation.

Peter, for example, was a character type who saw the world in terms of black and white, right and wrong. That's how he processed information. Moralistic, maintaining high personal standards of behavior, he felt strongly that all issues should be settled on merit; politics had no place in decisions. In a sense, there lay his blind spot.

The external reality piece: a diagnostic questionnaire

• Am I allowed to make my mark here?

You might find the "yes men" behavior of others, what Peter saw as sucking up to the chief, distasteful, obnoxious, offensive. But is it intended, in part, to diminish you? Not only do those individuals want to make themselves look good, but also they want to make you look bad?

If a clear-eyed external due diligence—being as nonjudmental, nonemotional as you can—convinces you that the politicians are out to undermine you, that's probably an environment you'll have to leave. However, let's say you just don't like or can't play politics, and you don't much like the coworkers who *are* playing it, but you're still recognized and approved for the quality of your work. Perhaps, then, you can quell your distaste enough to get on with the job.

• Are the popular people the best people for the job?

If the popular people are getting the rewards, do they deserve them?

This is not always so easy to figure out. Here, a few thoughts to ponder:

Employee X is a great individual contributor, a phenomenal performer, and just lousy with people. Despite his inadequate treatment of other human beings, the impact of his accomplishments on the organization is significant. Employee Y is a very good performer—not the best—and has excellent people skills. He's well-liked; he oils the interpersonal machinery of the organization in a way everyone appreciates. It might not be unfair or unjust if employee Y gets more in the way of rewards than does employee X.

Then we have employee A, a skilled performer whose interpersonal behavior is pretty good. He gets along with people. His coworker, employee B, is a favorite of the boss, who just loves him although B's technical or task performance is below standard. If employee B gets the fatter bonus, the bigger office, the higher raise than does employee A, that is probably unfair, unjust, and not equitable.

Peter decided two of the "yes men" in his unit were employee B types.

Putting together the internal and the external realities, what steps are available to Peter, the moralist?

Best next steps

- **Bide your time, while you seek greener pastures.**

Or some that suit you better. This is the conclusion that Peter would come to.

Given his natural difficulties managing the social piece of office life, combined with an atmosphere that encouraged "yes man" behavior, and considering a reward system that he believed was patently unfair, Peter decided he could not and would not fit into the organizational puzzle. He would move on.

Suppose you cannot accommodate to your highly politicized work environment in the ways we have suggested in this chapter. You find it impossible to reframe your attitudes; you don't want to conform to the behaviors, the appearances, and the styles of the people who win the prizes; you resent the need to network or to manage up more effectively. This is just not your personality or your preference, or consistent with your values.

If your dislike for playing politics as a key to success is that strong, it's probably time at least to begin considering other options. For example: Can you set up a consulting practice or establish your own business? Consulting or entrepreneurial work, while still inescapably somewhat political, is generally market driven, focused on responding to the needs of a customer and delivering a service. You are to a large extent freed from the hothouse atmosphere and the demands of life as a corporate citizen, where ego and personality can weigh so heavily towards getting ahead.

8

CONFUSED DIRECTIVES

HOW TO HANDLE MIXED SIGNALS FROM ABOVE

Confused directives can arrive in various ways. In whatever form, however, this seems to be one of the most common triggers of heightened anxiety in the office. The-powers-that-be send out signals that leave employees largely in the dark: What does that guy really want from me? What am I supposed to be doing? What is this company all about?

For example:

You're asked to work on multiple, overlapping projects that clearly conflict with each other.

Your manager gives you a real or symbolic pat on the back—a "nice work," a raise or unexpected bonus—and then in the next breath reduces the resources that enable you to do your job properly or eliminates some of the responsibilities for which you ostensibly received the pat on the back.

Between the time a new project is launched and the time it nears completion, management revises the stated objectives again and yet again, sending you and everyone working with you into a stressed-out, befuddled state.

Your organization takes the high road publicly—espousing elevated ethical standards, commitment to family, participation in community good works, and the like—but subtly punishes those employees who embrace it.

After your boss issues one set of instructions, it becomes clear that he misread the strategy or vision of *his* bosses. Top people are saying one thing; middle people are relaying an entirely different message to the troops.

What's causing the puzzlement, what it all means, is not always easy to determine. At the most basic level, however, we can distinguish between the innocent and the evil. Some confused directives come about out of relatively benign forces—a misunderstanding among levels of command, the temporary unavailability of pertinent information, a simple dearth of communication, or a somewhat incompetent communicator. Other mixed signals reflect forces that are not so benign at all, or a dishonest management playing both sides of the fence, possibly in a kind of passive aggressive strategy towards employees. Each situation calls for a different set of responses. In this chapter, we take a look at those possibilities, and what actions can help you ride out a turbulent tide:

- Honest confused directives—and how employees Jerry and Sally coped
- Dishonest confused directives—and how employee Todd coped

As you will see, many of the mixed signals, and the useful strategies to deal with them, somewhat echo the difficult boss scenarios presented in an earlier chapter. We do run into the good guy and the bad guy, or the temporarily overburdened guy and the two-faced guy. What's critical here is that the intensity of frustration and lowered morale that these office dilemmas usually produce can lead to a failure to achieve timely objectives. So this tricky workplace situation, more so than some of the others we've explored, can result in deteriorating performance from individuals and throughout a work unit.

How can you handle confused directives and mixed signals from above?

Jerry's story: what happened to him one day on the job

Jerry, 27, was a ninth-grade math teacher in a large suburban private school; his immediate supervisor was the upper school mathematics and science department head. In addition to teaching four classes a day, Jerry also led the after-school chess club and—wearing a couple of hats, as he liked to do—was the stage manager for an offshoot of the school drama group. He was a happily busy man. He became even busier though less happy when he began receiving a flurry of memos from his boss.

"Every time I checked my box," Jerry said, "there'd be another pile of notes from this guy. We've got to bring up the test scores, we've got to do more remedial work with the lower-performing kids, we've got to have interim reports. This might not have been so impossible to handle in itself, but then he'd pull a 180 on me. Completely reverse himself about something." At one point, the boss instructed Jerry to add a new study element in his classes over the following three months, and give him, the boss, feedback at the end of that period as to its success. About two weeks after delivering that mandate by memo, the boss stuck his head in Jerry's classroom at the end of the day and asked why he hadn't yet heard back from him about the study plan. "I pointed out that we were phasing this in over a three-month time frame, as he'd instructed," Jerry said, "and he didn't seem to register that. Now he wanted it done immediately."

Matters didn't improve. Jerry was told he'd have to disband the chess club and quit working with the drama group in order to devote after-class time to tutoring sessions. "I actually wondered if he was within his rights requiring me to do one-on-one work, but I did want to help some of these kids. Then the next thing I knew, he was loving the chess club and saying we had to start one in the middle school too, and I should get together with one of the teachers there and set it up. I never knew what I was going to hear next."

There was more paperwork to deal with, new forms to be filled out on a practically daily basis. Then the forms "seemed to go into the ozone; you never heard back about whether this information was useful or not." Jerry had the sense his boss wasn't even reading them. "I figured some of this hysteria was coming down from the new principal, this very highly touted educator who took over at the beginning of the year," he said. "We individual teachers didn't have that much contact with her; she liked to work through the department heads of the three divisions, the lower, middle, and upper schools. She seems to have some great ideas, actually. But it was up to my boss to smooth out the transition, get on top of that right away, and let the rest of us know exactly what was expected. That's his job."

Jerry was starting to dislike going into work in the morning. He was starting to dislike his boss—"I think the guy is kind of a weakling"—and avoided him as much as possible. He was ignoring some of the required paperwork. "The whole concept of burnout seemed real to me."

Sally's story: what happened to her one day on the job

"I love this job; I love what I do," said Sally, 48, "and I've put in a lot of years here. I really don't want to leave, but it's so upsetting, what's been happening." Sally was the manager of the better sportswear and casual clothes division in a large department store. She worked in a hyper environment at the best of times, supervising six to eight floor salespeople, consulting with the buyers, handling customer complaints, and overseeing the "personal shopper" service. Despite the pressures, she was a good worker. "I'm a little obsessive compulsive," she said. But her job and responsibilities were crystal clear in her mind. That was until the store entered negotiations for possible buyout by a large conglomerate, and nothing was so clear.

"I still have my budget, they haven't reduced my staff," Sally said. "But I don't know what management wants. On the one hand, I'm hearing, don't do anything yet because we're really not sure this or that is going to remain a priority. On the other hand, I'm expected to go ahead with business as usual." Everyone was aware of the impending sale of the store, but little up-to-date news was arriving about that. Sometimes Sally heard vague references to "a possible change in our vision for the future." When the new seasonal clothes were coming up and Sally sent her proposals to management, word came back that she was not to commit to certain lines "until we have further information." But at the same time, Sally said, "We're still running a store and I'm still running a women's clothing department, and I'm expected to get product out there on the floor and deliver business."

She was both confused and feeling pressured to perform, and her salespeople weren't helping. "I've been catching them just standing around talking among themselves, not paying proper attention to the customers. They can't do that. We just have to all work harder and keep going." The formerly hectic but smooth-running nature of Sally's day was rapidly deteriorating.

Schoolteacher Jerry and store manager Sally were feeling similarly at sea in terms of how they were to perform their jobs. Neither had any reason to suspect nefarious forces at the upper levels; these were not dishonest or nasty work environments. Each was encountering somewhat different circumstances and each needed to consider just what those were in order to shape the best responses.

The internal reality piece: a diagnostic questionnaire

Most employees, faced with mixed signals, will feel unsettled. Some are going to be more vulnerable and have more significant reactions, due to personal blind spots. If you are on the receiving end of confused directives, an internal reality investigation can shed light on the scene, and it might begin with a clear-eyed look at just how you are behaving—acting out—under the circumstances.

- **I'm not sure what I'm supposed to be doing, so what *am* I doing?**

    Is confusion causing you to:

    Fire off plaintive, annoyed, or sarcastic memos to management, requesting further information at once?

    Canvas coworkers repeatedly about what they're doing and how they're feeling, and engage in hourly gripe sessions?

    Drag your feet, ignore directives that don't make sense, and avoid the people who are issuing them?

    This was essentially how Jerry was starting to act out on his feelings of frustration. "The man has no idea what he wants," Jerry said about his supervisor, "let him figure that out and then come tell me. Meantime, I'll deal with my kids and my classes the way I want to."

    Or is confusion and anxiety causing you to put up blinkers, keep your head down, and barrel forward as always, while everyone around you continues to feel in an ever-increasing pressure cooker?

    There's a lot to be said for barreling forward as always, as Sally was, but that can also produce a kind of obliviousness to some of the more subtle needs and developments in the office.

    It's not too difficult to identify behaviors that, while understandable in emotional terms, are clearly not productive and forward-looking. Anxiety—which, of course, can express itself is so many ways—can lead to any such reactions, but they need to be managed and reined in. So the internal reality investigation continues with a look at where all that anxiety is coming from.

- **Am I getting more anxious than maybe the situation warrants?**

Why might that be?

Toning down the level of your anxiety, getting your emotions under control, taming that tiger, opens you up to taking a more reasoned appraisal of the situation and deciding what options you have—or if there's anything you can do to help minimize the confusion. Certain personality types and/or childhood experiences can predispose one to be hit hard by mixed signals. So think about the following:

Do you typically require a high degree of clarity and consistency in your day-to-day life in order to perform well? Consequently, you bristle at, worry over, resent, or become unraveled by any hint of ambiguity? Is that your blind spot?

On her job, Sally was unable to plan ahead in a realistic way, because management was not telling her whether or not her world would be the same in six months. That would create some degree of tension in anybody, but doubly so in someone like Sally with a tendency to become overwhelmed within an atmosphere of uncertainty. She perceived no way to operate other than as she always had, just "work harder." She was able to trace that behavior back to her school days. "I wasn't the smartest student, but I got good grades because I put in more hours doing homework than anybody else. Like I said, I'm sort of an obsessive compulsive, and whatever assignments the teachers gave, I just worked at it until I got it done."

Are you a generally impatient individual?

Jerry might place somewhere along this continuum. Certainly, there was no question he was receiving mixed signals about procedures. But his work wasn't being called into question, he wasn't in danger of losing his job, and significantly, he could identify the arrival of a new principal as a factor that was probably stirring up the pot. Maybe Jerry was one who didn't cope well with the relatively elongated process of shifting into new strategies or directions. He had a somewhat high sense of urgency about the whole situation; his boss *should* have ironed out any kinks right away, was Jerry's thought. When the boss wasn't doing that, Jerry was ready to write him off.

Or, do you place a high value on order and maintaining a sense of control over your destiny?

If you grew up in a chaotic household as a child, and you learned early on that you and you alone could ensure that life ran relatively smoothly, perhaps now as an adult you're particularly vulnerable when outside forces disrupt a previously regimented routine.

Would you call yourself an outcome-oriented achiever, a type A, someone who feels successful only when a project is driven through from beginning to end and thwarted or frustrated when circumstances make that impossible?

Are you more of a follower than a leader?

There's no sin in being a follower. No blame to not being a leader. Organizations need some of both. But people who are not particularly independent, who rely heavily on external authority for specific guidelines, can be seriously thrown off track when straightforward instructions are not issued. Then, it's impossible to reach a decision about taking any productive action at all.

There's nothing *wrong* with these modes of functioning in general. However, they can make life harder and nerves more frayed when confused directives are impacting the work environment. Try to define your natural predispositions and how they may be influencing your emotions, and you'll be in a stronger position to manage both your feelings and the reactions they are producing.

• What's my goal here?

In the midst of a period of uncertainty, it's a helpful idea to refocus one's sights on the ultimate objectives, whatever those might be. It can be all too tempting to dissipate energies and use up time carping, even if only to oneself, about the dysfunctional, know-nothing, crazy, weakling losers who are running the place. Refocus.

Aside from, probably, holding on to your job, what's your main goal?

Jerry might need to remind himself: I want to feel not distracted and distanced from my primary objective, which is teaching and coaching children. Sally might need to tell herself: I want to maintain a stable atmosphere in my sales group and take care of our customers.

Once you've tamed your tigers, an exploration of the external reality in your workplace should suggest the best ways to cope. Specifically, you will uncover what positive influences you might be able to exert or you will realize, in fact, there's not a whole lot you can do to change the confused directives.

The external reality piece: a diagnostic questionnaire

Here's the first question:

• Does my boss or management actually *know* what's going on?

In other words, decide you need to figure out how possible and practical it is for those in charge to deliver the goods right now. Can your boss or company management reasonably be expected to convey full, timely, candid, and factual information that will dispel the ambiguity or confusion?

If the answer is yes—boss/management knows what's going on and has information they actually would like you to have in order to perform your work—there is a problem in communication. This individual or these people are somewhat incompetent or inadequate in their managerial role. If the answer is no—boss/management probably does not have the information that would ease your discomfort at the moment—improving communication is not a top priority. It's not theirs, and it shouldn't be yours.

To discern the reality of the situation, the following bit of due diligence might help:

- **Has there been a history or pattern of inadequate or incompetent communication?**

  If you have any kind of track record with your organization and/or immediate supervisor, you'll probably have no trouble with the answer to that one. We'll assume here that your manager's mixed signals are not just par for the course, the typical stuff going on in a chronically chaotic environment, but rather, temporarily aberrant behaviors. Normally, office life has been proceeding pretty smoothly, with everybody getting the picture. This is good to remember. It suggests that current influences are upsetting the scene, and maybe you can discover what those are and do something about them.

- **Is this organization in a time of flux at the moment?**

  When major developments are underway—there's a possible merger afoot, a move to a new facility is planned, and so on—it can be considered normal and even appropriate that directives coming from above are confusing, not fully fleshed-out, or subject to change without much notice. Mixed signals are the unintentional effects of an organization in transition. Recent anticipated or unanticipated developments are causing management to adjust vision and/or strategies. They can't, so to speak, be blamed for confusing you.

- **Can I influence events in a helpful way at this point?**

    Is it in your capacity or power to take actions to clear up the fog?

    Perhaps you will realize that while you cannot control events entirely, you *can* work on the communication angle, both in the way you are receiving communications and the way you are sending them out.

Best next steps

- **Manage up, if appropriate, to come to the aid of a supervisor in trouble.**

    Suppose you have concluded that you're dealing with an incompetent or inadequate communicator, the mostly good guy boss under stress. You're giving management the benefit of the doubt; you believe they'd do a better job at conveying directives if they only knew how.

    Without making the boss look stupid or causing him to feel bad, offer ideas and actions that might help produce a semblance of stability and consistency in the office. In a nonjudgmental, supportive manner, suggest measures to improve the flow of communication. Or, help him better translate messages that *he's* receiving.

    After comparing notes with some of his fellow teachers, Jerry realized that the new principal was obviously trying to light a fire under everybody and that his own boss, the department head, was probably feeling overburdened to the max. He decided to give the man a break. He told himself, in effect: "Yes, I'm annoyed, this situation bothers me, but I can do something about it by helping my boss out. I know a little of what's been going on throughout the school because of a new principal changing the landscape and shaking things up." He decided to manage his boss, very carefully.

    In a quiet and undistracted moment, Jerry told his boss:

    "I can tell there's a lot of stress going on; you've been told to implement a number of new directives, and this is a tough period of adjustment. Because of that, however, you're inadvertently and unintentionally providing information that can be very confusing. Can I help you with this?"

Jerry had come prepared with three specific ideas, including the suggestion that he and the boss have a brief, scheduled check-in twice a week—"just so I can be sure we're on the same page and I'm clear about your expectations." The boss was receptive.

There's not always the opportunity to manage up. For example, Sally realized she wasn't working for an incompetent communicator, but for a group in transition. She told herself, in effect: "I'd like more clarity. I always like to be given assignments. I know I'm vulnerable to the lack of information from above, but I can't have an impact there. Management is not failing to communicate because they think it's not important; they are riding through corporate developments that are still in flux."

• Manage down to reduce the confusion of subordinates.

If you have a leadership role, even with one subordinate, and if you are receiving no clear directives and you're feeling abandoned and without moorings, think of this as a growth opportunity. You'd like more support, more guidance, but it's not forthcoming; so in the meantime take the initiative to reduce your level of anxiety, and behave courageously and effectively with the person or people who are looking to *you* for support and guidance.

For example, adding to the difficulties mounting in her department was the fact that Sally was in charge of supervising the floor salespeople. And those individuals were all keenly aware that major changes were coming down the pike, with perhaps negative effects on their unit. Would they survive or not? Were people going to be out of jobs?

Sally needed to realize she wasn't managing her staff very well, and that was something she *could* influence. She needed to meet with her employees and provide them with as much information and direction as was feasible from her own awareness and within corporate confidentiality standards. She might say:

"Look, I need to be straightforward with you. There are mixed signals right now because of potential changes in the future. I can't give you all the news you would like, because I don't have it. When I know more about what's happening, you will know. I realize this is unsettling. In the meantime, this is what we can do. . . ."

• **Go with the flow.**

Here's another personal growth opportunity. And this calls for some conscious thought and determination.

Take the long view and go with the flow. Be patient. Work on yourself to lessen a possibly overblown need for predictability. Figure that for a likely period of three to six months your work routine will be impacted by confused directives and mixed signals, but you will cope.

It just might be a chance to grow into a more mature person, to accept the fact that you will not always obtain the outcome you want and within the time frame you desire. It just might be a time for self-reflection, time to sit back and ponder how you typically react to what the office and life in general hands you. Maybe the environment is doing you a favor by requiring you to slow down, go with the flow, and realize the limits of your control. Some of my clients, in fact, riding out a time of mixed signals, have concluded they're too aggressive, too type A, and they haven't been doing their health any good!

Todd's story: what happened to him one day on the job

Todd, 36, had some inkling that his company, where he'd worked for two years, wasn't quite as high-minded as they made themselves out to be. His organization was a large consulting firm providing technology support to major corporations. "This place likes to present itself as cutting edge when it comes to treating their employees well, very concerned with work-and-family balance issues, and also very caring about the world at large," Todd said, "They have a motto: 'Our service is technology, our business is people.' They give contributions to fund-raisers for good causes, but it tends to be the high profile, sexy ones, where there's publicity in it. You see a picture in the paper the next day of the chief in a tux at a fancy dinner."

He'd noticed a disconnect between the image and the reality. "I've been here long enough to see that these guys who run the place don't always walk the talk. They're really all about the bottom line, and not so nice when anything gets in the way of that."

These inklings came into sharp focus when Todd opted to take advantage of a policy providing for flex-time and telecommuting. His wife was changing jobs; they had two young children, and it made sense for Todd to work out of the home for a while. Practically speaking, he could do so, because as one of the organization's senior support technicians he was able to handle most of his work by phone and computer. Politically speaking, he didn't see a problem, because his high level of expertise was recognized and valued.

So Todd arranged for a six-month stretch during which he worked on-site three days a week and out of his home two days. Management approved; there would be no negative fallout, he was assured by his boss, as long as his results were good. A highly disciplined and organized individual, he had the office/home situation flowing smoothly within a couple of weeks of getting the plan underway, though it meant pushing himself. On his three days in the office, he was putting in 12 hours at a stretch.

Business was good throughout the organization, and during those six months Todd responded to even more client calls than he had the year before. He delivered, with increased revenue and positive evaluations from his customers. Nevertheless, though his results were higher, his year-end bonus was substantially less than his previous one.

He was furious. "I got duped. The only reason I can see for getting shortchanged is that they really didn't like me working from home. Which they told me at the start was not a problem. Which they supposedly are all in favor of, because they care so much about the well-being of their employees and families. It was a crock."

Where could Todd go from there?

The kinds of mixed signals we're talking about here do fall into that gray zone. If this is your particular tricky office situation, you perceive you are working for a company that doesn't "walk the talk." Management takes admirable positions on social issues, let's say, while demonstrating in various ways that in fact they don't exactly honor them. Perhaps, as in Todd's case, certain generous programs are ostensibly valued and employees will be treated respectfully if they choose to participate. Turns out they aren't so treated. That's hypocrisy.

But a hypocritical organization, one in which management behaviors on a day-to-day basis regarding individual employees pointedly conflict with their stated policies, is not necessarily doing anything illegal. What *you* do about the situation usually revolves around a couple of questions:

How much does a hypocritical environment bother you mentally or emotionally?

How much is it impacting you practically?

If you think it has impacted you practically—the decreased bonus, the passed-over promotion, for example—you might end up challenging a management action or decision, which won't be easy. So be sure you're reading the signals right. Conduct your internal and external explorations with care.

The internal reality piece: a diagnostic questionnaire

Todd needed above all to contain his fury about being "derailed."

- **Have I been acting out in a negative way because of negative signals?**

    When you believe you have been handed a line of goods—given to understand that the organization you're working for applauds certain altruistic or family-centered practices and then it seems, in reality, they don't—the natural reaction is one of anger. You might feel you have been lied to, betrayed, or penalized unjustly. Maybe you have. But you do not want to behave in any way that threatens your job. You want to cool down in order to think clearly and plan your next steps.

- **Have I been building up a list of grievances?**

    And so possibly jumping to conclusions about the mixed signals?

    Consider whether you've been quietly seething for a long time about the way the place is being run in general. And now this latest development, which directly affects you, was the final straw. And you are convinced at once that it can be chalked up to a corrupt management.

    Be careful. Don't let a rush to judgment stop you from conducting your due diligence.

- **Am I deeply disgusted by the duplicitous nature of this organization?**

    The question really has to do with personal issues of character, integrity, morality, or religious beliefs. If you are, in fact, strongly bothered by the disconnect between values that are important to you and the behaviors of your organization, there might come a time you must weigh those feelings against your need for the job.

The external reality piece: a diagnostic questionnaire

- ### Are the mixed signals I received a reflection of the company culture?

Clearly, it's important to determine if there's a pattern of hypocrisy in management practices or if, unfortunately, you're working under confused directives because you are being singled out for torment. (If you are being singled out for torment, perhaps because your supervisors are hoping to ease you out the door, the following chapter—mission impossible—has strategies you should know.)

Keep your ears open and your radar alert to pick up clues that reflect the moral underpinnings of the organization. You might have a sense of that already. You might learn more from coworkers.

- ### Have others experienced mixed signals of a similar sort?

Discreetly, take a reading of a few trusted coworkers, if at all possible. This is the population, after all, that has been functioning under the same umbrella as you and presumably has made observations as well.

For example, Todd looked around, asked around, and heard a couple of stories that seemed to corroborate his impressions of a consistent pattern of hypocrisy. "I knew one of the other men in my division, a brilliant guy and an excellent worker, had been counting on a bump up to senior level, and then he got passed over for the promotion. He and I went out for a beer after work, started talking, and he's convinced he didn't get the promotion because he took the corporate-sponsored, executive volunteer sabbatical, where he was loaned to a nonprofit for a couple of months. In fact, when he was back and when the promotion possibility was coming up, his boss told him flat out that they felt he wasn't putting in enough time and energy on the job. And this is even though they supposedly admire employees for doing these good works!"

Another coworker told Todd that although the organization provided on-site emergency day care, she was subtly made to feel uncomfortable by her boss whenever she brought her child to the office. After two such experiences, she decided it wasn't wise to take advantage of the day care program.

He also learned that bonuses had not been slashed across the board, because of lowered company earnings. His reduced bonus had to do just with him, it seemed.

Todd's investigation convinced him that he was right about the mixed signals from management. Despite the company's stated support of certain principles, when push came to shove they denigrated or devalued employees.

Best next steps

- **Develop your psychological protective coating.**

Or a chameleonlike cover. Emotionally detach from the work environment. When you have assessed that you're dealing with hypocritical people, you can't allow your emotions to be shredded because of it.

This is a form of office politics, and, as we explored in the previous chapter, each individual must decide how much he's willing to put up with, before the putting-up-with begins to disturb personal values and ethics. If you need the job you have, see no alternative options at the moment, then do what you must do to get by and manage the contradictions, as long as you are not asked to become involved in anything illegal.

Try that for a while. If you can't be that kind of person, or don't want to be that kind of person, then you truly do have to find employment elsewhere sooner or later.

• Present your concerns to the boss.

Todd believed he merited a larger bonus and the reason he did not receive it was because he had opted to work from his home for much of the previous year. This was an allegation that, of course, he could not prove. (He would have been in a stronger position had he requested, at the initial discussion of the revised work plan, a memo from the boss describing the alternative job arrangement and what impact it would have on his bonus.) But he could voice his concerns. Ideally, he would have kept a diary on his earlier discussions with management, which he could refer to in the talk with his boss, and would also have documented evidence of outstanding performance.

Without making accusations of hypocrisy, without referring to "all the other employees I know this place has treated unfairly," Todd might say:

"We did discuss my telecommuting arrangement. I was assured that my adjusted work schedule would have no negative repercussions. My performance over the period in question exceeded my previous performance, as these several measures show. However, my bonus has been cut substantially. I am wondering if my not being in the office had something to do with that."

There's a chance Todd might get his improved bonus. There's a chance he might not.

• Look at the avenues for internal concerns.

When you're convinced you have been unfairly penalized and you have received no satisfaction after your first-level discussions, you do have the option of presenting your concerns to HR. But before you do so, be very clear in your own mind whether you are seeking advice on how to proceed or you are prepared to present a grievance. There's a difference. (See the information on HR, page 29, for suggestions.)

Todd might decide his next best step is sit down with the company's HR professional and ask for advice: "I have concerns about the level of my bonus and I feel I have been treated unfairly. I have talked to my management and I'm not satisfied with the response I received. Before I turn this into a grievance, I'd like to know, did I handle this appropriately or is there anything else I can do?" He then will explain in detail the nature of his concerns, including the discussions with his boss.

If Todd felt justified in presenting a grievance—which step essentially compels HR to pursue the matter—his conversation is somewhat different: "I am concerned that I've been discriminated against and treated unfairly. Before I go outside, I want to talk to you, ask if you can investigate, and see if there is a way to remedy this situation. I would rather work inside than outside the system."

Then give HR or other internal resources a chance.

If HR cannot be helpful or you feel the help they give you is not enough, and you have exhausted all internal resources, there is nothing wrong with seeking a consultation with a private attorney.

• Consult with a private attorney.

If Todd can find an attorney with some knowledge of his organization, one who perhaps has heard complaints from other employees, that lawyer may be able to offer him sophisticated advice on how to re-approach management to get what he wants, the appropriate bonus. (See the information on lawyers on page 44.) Or, the attorney might be invaluable in helping Todd negotiate a positive way of leaving the organization.

That last is a possibility for which he should be ready.

When you reach this level of confrontation—you have decided to fight the effects of the mixed signals sent by a hypocritical organization—be prepared to leave.

9

MISSION IMPOSSIBLE

HOW TO FIND MIDDLE-GROUND SOLUTIONS
(OR RECOGNIZE WHEN YOU'RE BEING
SET UP FOR THE KILL)

Your desk is buried under a mound of paperwork, you have two dozen little pink sticky notes indicating phone calls you still must return, the temp help you requested hasn't materialized—and the boss hands you yet another project with yet another "ASAP!!" written on the top.

Various developments and various types of bosses seem to generate these mission impossible scenes, but recognizing two broad categories is useful in figuring out the most adaptive responses to them. We come again to the matter of intent—and the innocent and the evil, or the benign and the not so benign. In the first eventuality, the boss/management is naive or uninformed and thus largely unaware of the impact of heavy demands on employees. Once made to understand what is reasonable or realistic and what isn't, ideally he'll change his tune and do right—or better—by his workers. In the second eventuality, the boss/management knows quite well that his expectations are over the top, but the misery of employees doesn't seem to bother him. Either this individual views staff primarily as useful tools for his own advancement *or* he is intentionally turning the screws, creating such an intolerable situation that his employee will up and leave under her own steam or will present performance problems sufficiently serious to be fired.

Either case—surviving the mission impossible or getting out without losing your shirt—calls for the fine art of negotiation.

In the following two scenarios, we consider those strategies:

- The innocent mission impossible—and how employee Kathryn coped
- The intentional mission impossible—and how employee Eric coped

Again, personal blind spots heighten vulnerabilities and can lead to a completely frustrating, unsatisfactory, or even damaging outcome.

Kathryn's story: what happened to her one day on the job

She had been at the job for half a year, said Kathryn, 52, "and lately I feel like crying every afternoon. There's so much work, it's impossible for me to keep up." Kathryn had been hired as executive assistant to the associate director of a statewide food distribution service for low-income clients. Her boss, 35-year-old Brad, had been director for a little over a year. "Brad has his eye on the future," she said, "and he's spending more time on corporate and foundation relations, fund-raising and so on. I know that's smart. It's good for the organization, good for him personally. He'll probably move to the national office eventually."

Kathryn had no complaints about Brad as a human being, and even as a boss, in most respects. "He really is dedicated to the kind of work we do. I get caught up in his enthusiasm for the mission. At least I did in the beginning. I just feel overwhelmed."

She had good reason. Kathryn's job required disseminating information about the organization's programs, coordinating efforts among community groups, drafting grant applications, and arranging and overseeing volunteer staff, in addition to maintaining her boss's schedule and correspondence. Working out of a cramped office, Kathryn had limited—and decreasing—physical resources. There were two copying machines, but only one had been working for the past several months. Her two-person clerical staff had been reduced to one when a woman on maternity leave elected not to return and wasn't replaced.

But one development brought her to that point of burnout. "We've had a person coming into the office a couple of days a week lately, a statistician who's working on a special survey. And he said to me the first week, 'I won't be hiring an assistant, so Brad said I could share you; hope you don't mind.' He's very nice, like Brad, but neither of them seems to realize that I just can't handle all this."

Kathryn was a competent employee, and a veteran worker. She'd been an administrative assistant in a number of organizations for many years. She had legitimate reasons to be feeling put-upon. Yet she kept on taking it and taking it. She needed to figure out why.

The internal reality piece: a diagnostic questionnaire

These workplace dilemmas do present tricky situations. After all, you've been hired to do a job and you're expected to do it, and you might not be quite certain you're entitled to gripe about what's being handed to you. However, as a sane, relatively experienced corporate citizen, you are able to draw your line in the sand and realize when you are, indeed, being overloaded. If, then, you're still not speaking up, why might that be? What's stopping you? Consider:

• Do I go to any lengths to avoid what I anticipate must be a confrontation?

Are you bending under the increasing burden of a mission impossible because it's just too difficult to say "no"? Too uncomfortable to think about trying to arrange a middle-ground, more sensible work picture for yourself?

And why do you believe that presenting your concerns must inevitably be "a confrontation," with its connotation of something unpleasant and attack-like, where one side wins and one side loses? It's true. Sometimes there is no room for negotiation—for a win-win—but this is rarely the case when a valued worker demonstrates why she is bordering on burnout.

• Do I have a problem with authority figures when it comes to saying my piece?

You feel you must comply with any and every request from on high, regardless of the personal cost you pay?

These issues often have roots in childhood. Some people who take the obedient path in difficult office situations, who can't say no, unconsciously feel guilty, "bad," and deserving of poor treatment, even punishment. Perhaps overly critical parents or an unforgiving culture or religion planted such notions early on. There might be a fear of not pleasing, not being liked or loved.

Kathryn had no difficulty spotting these tendencies in herself. She'd been aware of them for a long time, actually. "I always have to be the good girl, the one who doesn't complain. I have absolutely no doubt it's because of how I grew up, with a very strict father and a quiet, repressed mother. My sister and I would do anything to avoid making my father angry." Her blind spot seemed especially obvious in this latest job, "where my boss is almost young enough to be my son. And I'm being the obedient daughter who doesn't make waves!" Down deep, even without realizing it, Kathryn might have assumed greater age meant greater power; perhaps a trace of resentment at having to do the unrealistic bidding of a youthful boss added to her frustration.

If you're in the grip of any such emotions, clearly you might need to work up your courage factor and steel yourself to take an action that is naturally difficult for you, which is probably to point out to the boss that your workload has become intolerable and relief is desperately required. It helps to remember that this individual isn't a father or a mother, and that a need to be loved doesn't really have a place in the office.

The external reality piece: a diagnostic questionnaire

While you are working up the courage factor, review any mitigating circumstances that might have contributed to the stressed-out state of affairs.

- **Is the boss/management aware that I'm overloaded?**

Start on an upbeat note, and assume the boss doesn't realize the depth of the pressures he's been putting you under. If he *did* realize, he'd take measures to alleviate them, because he's a decent manager. So:

Are there signs that my supervisor is a little clueless?

Are there understandable reasons why he might be?

For example, maybe the boss is simply not around much. His own work requirements take him out in the field and mean that you and he don't actually see each other very often. By the time you arrive in the morning, he's come and gone, leaving a fresh stack of paperwork on your desk.

Or, he's distracted by the need to prove himself reasonably quickly to the people *he* reports to, and that's made him a bit oblivious. Maybe he's caught in his own mission impossibles.

Or, he "has his eye on the future," the bigger picture, and doesn't recognize the time and resources required to keep up with the more mundane or supportive services the bigger picture requires. He's a good motivator, he conveys his enthusiasm for the work, and he doesn't think about the rest.

Or, perhaps you, unwittingly, have been contributing to his obliviousness by maintaining a stiff upper lip and a grim smile, saying nothing, delivering the impossible tasks—although you're a basket case of exhaustion and desperation at the end of every seemingly endless day.

So maybe he is unaware of what's been happening with you, and getting more information on the table is just what's needed at this point.

• Is there an immediate crisis in the office?

How long has the mission impossible been going on?

Clearly, if a rush job has arisen—a major report is due in three months, people have been pulled off their usual assignments, regular work is piling up—that's a piece of the picture that should shape some of your argument. If you know the situation has a finite life span and the end will be in sight before too long, you have a bargaining chip in a sense, as we see below.

Best next steps

Kathryn, after her internal reality analysis and self-talk, ideally will have mentally replaced the notion of a nasty confrontation with the notion of a civilized negotiation, which is much more pleasant. In any negotiation:

- **Assume a satisfactory outcome.**

Think positively. Especially if you have great difficulty saying no, if you are afraid of being unloved and not a "good girl" anymore, talk yourself into a more optimistic frame of mind. Bestow on the boss power and respect by believing that he has not been intending to overburden you and that he has simply not considered the consequences of his unrealistic expectations. Give him the opportunity to understand.

Assume he will respond with some version of, "You're right. We have a problem. Let's put our heads together and come up with a plan."

- **Marshall information that demonstrates the downside to the demands you are asked to meet.**

Prepare your script. You want to appeal on the basis of facts, not emotions, and help management see that continuing at the current pace might very well lead to less productive employees, a less polished product, the possibility of making errors in the work, or whatever the downside might be.

Kathryn, for example, needs to explain to her boss, Brad, the negative fallout of what's being required of her. Then she must solicit his support by outlining priorities that make more sense. So before approaching him with any such discussion, she must think out carefully what the downside is in terms of how she is currently attempting to achieve the organization's goals.

- **Educate the boss.**

Approaching the boss in a supportive manner—without coming across as judgmental, angry, resentful, or suggesting that he doesn't know what he's doing, without putting him on the defensive or sounding pathetic—explain the circumstances that you have scripted in your mind beforehand. Convey the attitude that you wish above all to help resolve problems. Be a problem solver, not simply a problem identifier. Kathryn might begin by saying something like:

"I want to perform at the level you expect. I want to support you. I can appreciate what you'd like me to achieve, and I understand there are demands on you also. For some time now, however, my workload has been difficult to sustain. I am working 12 and 13 hours most days, but even so I'm still not addressing all our needs properly. I have some suggestions on what we need to maintain our level of productivity. Part of the difficulty has been reduced resources, and you might not be aware of what those are. Let me explain them to you. They include. . . ."

She then mentions the inadequate office equipment, the loss of her clerical support staff, and the shared-time arrangement with the statistician who has no assistant. Demonstrating an awareness of cost and budgetary limitations will show Brad that she understands some of his management issues. She discusses hiring another staff individual, replacing nonfunctioning machines, and possibly reducing the number of assignments she has been given.

• Propose a short-term period of adaptation.

In the course of this kind of negotiation, management perhaps will offer feedback regarding the length of the mission impossible situation. If, indeed, there's a relatively short-term crisis that must be met, perhaps it's not unreasonable that everyone will be expected to struggle under demanding conditions for a while.

On the other hand, if it's not so much a temporary turn of events, but a more persistent state of affairs, there has to be either a change in expectations, an increase in resources, or a shift in priorities.

Depending on the outcome of their talk, Kathryn might say to her boss: "I would like to be able to continue at this pace, and I can do it for a period of time, but if the pressures don't ease along the lines we've talked about, I would like to discuss the situation with you again in two months."

So after all this, what can you expect? The external reality due diligence and the steps I've described here are not only potentially curative—you are able to bring about an improved picture to your work life—but diagnostic. For example: Suppose you've done everything right, you've approached the boss in an empathetic manner and with a genuine wish to educate him, and you have outlined your needs and the accommodations you are prepared to make in the short term. You behaved well. And the boss responded, in so many words or through his actions in the near future, with some version of: "Tough luck. I don't especially care that you're overburdened. If you don't like it you can leave." You have diagnosed a much trickier situation, possibly even the intentional mission impossible in which you are being set up to fail.

We explore these developments in the following scenario.

Eric's story: what happened to him one day on the job

Eric, 34, was a communications specialist in the public relations department of a pharmaceutical company. His boss, the assistant vice president for PR, was "a pit bull," in Eric's words, "you don't get in her way if she's in a bad mood and you'd like to keep your skin." Having worked for her for almost four years, Eric had come to perceive her as not a terribly likable human being. "She's single-minded, a careerist. If you give her what she wants, she won't bother you. She'll never give you any praise, but she won't get on your case. That's all right. I don't have to like her."

For the past three or four months, however, the boss did seem to be getting on Eric's case. He was aware, as was everyone in the organization, of one of the periodic cost-cutting waves washing through the corporation. Recent FDA regulations had delayed the scheduled release of a new product, quarterly earnings were down, and the crunch was on. Several positions had not been filled after attrition left them vacated, including two people in Eric's division. At the same time, Eric's boss made it clear she expected the same level of delivery from her employees. Eric's workload had grown alarmingly, and with the reduced staff, he could barely keep up.

But other developments were leaving him increasingly uneasy. "I wasn't getting the usual feedback from the boss, for one thing. She had to sign off on my memos or reports, and that was typically a routine procedure, a quick turnaround. Now I had to pin her down to get my approvals, and sometimes that would take three or four days. So I was losing time and that was impacting the work, while simultaneously she was piling it on."

Eric had "a vague sense I was being intentionally stymied." He decided he had to confirm or dismiss his suspicions before he could do anything about his predicament.

The internal reality piece: a diagnostic questionnaire

We talked earlier about the obedient employee, the one who just can't say no and will take on the burden of an impossible situation in order to avoid a confrontation. Those personality types will almost certainly be more vulnerable to the behaviors of the ambitious or destructive boss. But other blind spots can also interfere with an adaptive response. Ask yourself:

• Am I a perfectionist?

Some people are so driven by work and ambition that they impose upon themselves excessively high standards about what they should achieve. Unconsciously, they mirror the unrealistic expectations of management. And so despite laboring under a mission impossible and enormous stress, the perfectionist will try to rise to the occasion. His boss's goals become his. Unable to see the forest for the trees, he might easily push himself to the point of collapse. Burnout is real and a threat to oneself.

- **When a boss/management is behaving unreasonably, do I automatically assume evil motives?**

Other individuals tend to perceive all authority figures in a malignant light. They're suspicious; they believe management is of course an opposing and hurtful force, out to get them. Often, that's a response found in victims of parental abuse or betrayal. The difficulty is, assuming evil motives leads to reacting defensively or even aggressively, without attempting any rapprochement. In these cases your faulty assumptions might turn out to be the biggest part of your perceived problems.

So these are questions to mull over as you try to keep your emotions under control and think carefully through your next moves.

The external reality piece: a diagnostic questionnaire

The immediate challenge is to discern just what manner of creature you're dealing with: Is the boss an ambitious, out-for-herself individual who's probably aware of the stress she's causing her staff, but doesn't much care? Or are you in the middle of a more sinister plot, in which a destructive management intends to axe or eliminate the positions of some employees by forcing them out—apparently by accepting their voluntary resignations?

In the first eventuality, you have a chance of improving the picture. In the second, you might find yourself in a thornier negotiation entirely. Time for some due diligence.

- **What's the history?**

Has management previously gone about cost cutting or downsizing in an indirect manner, one in which an employee or two has been blindsided and found herself out the door without quite realizing what happened? That kind of history suggests an organization with little concern for individual well-being.

- **Does other data seem to support the notion that I'm being set up?**

Aside from a task overload:

Have you been excluded from meetings you previously attended, in what looks like a systematic effort to keep you out of the loop?

You've been denied a bonus, or received a more restricted one? Or have you not had a salary raise?

Memos or reports you send out are not responded to, or are returned with a blunt "needs further work?"

Has your title been demoted?

In fact, some of this was exactly what Eric was experiencing. "More and more I was reading the handwriting on the wall," he said, "I knew there was a push to reduce staff. I was pretty sure I was right in thinking that my boss was intentionally marginalizing me in various ways. I didn't get a year-end raise. Simultaneously, she was swamping me with so much work that it was almost inevitable I'd start not producing as well as before." He also figured that, as a highly paid specialist, "it would obviously be a lot cheaper for the company if they could fire me for performance or if I just quit."

Eric did a little sleuthing. "My boss's executive assistant is a friend of mine, and I asked her if she'd heard any scuttlebutt. Turns out, the boss has met with a consultant who's making recommendations for reorganization, including outsourcing a couple of jobs to an independent contractor. Of course, that would make sense in my case. Eliminate my benefits, change a fixed cost into a variable cost, and hire somebody who can do an adequate enough job for much less money."

So the handwriting was definitely on the wall, Eric decided. He was right to be suspect about the security of his job.

Best next steps

Let's assume you have *not* uncovered clues that management is suggesting you take a walk, to some other job. But all indications point to a supervisor who's only interested in her employee's ability to further her own career. Time to have a talk. In this mission impossible situation, negotiation takes a different slant than the one we explored regarding Kathryn and her essentially sympathetic but unaware supervisor.

• Approach the boss by tending to her ego.

The ambitious, unsympathetic manager isn't going to be motivated to change by the news that her staff is overloaded and unhappy. What is *more likely* to get her attention is the possibility that her employees will fail to meet company expectations—and thus *she* will look bad. So the solution here is not so much to educate the boss, but to appeal to her ego and sense of self-preservation, and to convince her that as much as you do want to deliver, alas, the work might not get done.

Point out that extreme issues are leading to a mission failure that will reflect poorly not only on you but on her as well. The conversation goes something like the following:

"I think you know that I'm strongly committed to your success. However, there are demonstrated problems, and I need your help in order to maintain your success and avoid failure. I don't see any way of working myself, or the rest of the staff, harder than we're already working. There are signs of real burnout in the department, declining performance, and reduced quality in the service. We're having a lot of absenteeism. People are getting sick. We simply don't have enough time and resources to get the job done, and our quotas are not going to be met. You need to know that. And I hope you do know this worrisome situation we're in is not because of my not wanting to try."

The aim is to make it clear that desired goals cannot be achieved.

There will be a meltdown. When her own performance and reputation is on the line, this boss will take action to protect herself—even if it means helping her workers.

If you're in Eric's predicament, however, and reliably convinced that you are being pressured out of a job, the conversation should take a more deliberate turn.

• Ask for clarification.

For example, Eric can approach his boss, as described above, in a nonthreatening, not angry or emotional manner, and state that he's been put in a situation that will not lead to success. He describes some of the demonstrated problems in the department. Then he adds:

"I have to say, I'm puzzled and confused. I did not receive my expected increase in salary. I have been excluded from departmental meetings lately, which has made it difficult for me to keep abreast of developments I need to know in order to do my job properly. I've been given a great deal more work than before. So I'm concerned what this is all about. Can you clarify my situation for me?"

He listens to what the boss has to say, and he's likely to hear one of three responses.

One: "Okay, yeah Eric, you got me, I have to reduce staff and I'm going to eliminate your job. You know what? I'm ready to negotiate something for you." So Eric might find himself in the middle of job elimination with discussions regarding severance.

Two: "I don't know what you're talking about. We're in a cost cutting mode, and you just have to work as hard as it takes to get your job done. So get back to it." Eric is sent away with his boss offering nothing by way of clarification or accommodation, and, in addition, seemingly blaming him for a lackadaisical performance.

Three: "Well, Eric, it sounds like you're just not very happy here. Are you telling me you're turning in your resignation? Sorry to see you go." Eric receives further proof that he's working for a company that would like him out and doesn't want to pay him anything on the way.

The first possibility may, in some ways, be the easiest—or the most straightforward—to handle. Finding yourself discussing separation from the organization can be a shock, but if it's one you have been anticipating and/or dreading, the shock might be accompanied by a degree of relief. It might be an improvement over working away under a cloud of worry and uncertainty. And depending on your circumstances, you might be in a position to negotiate a severance package to your satisfaction.

If you are met with "I don't know what you're talking about" or "I accept your resignation," your best next steps are difficult.

• Keep up your work, while you seek appropriate advice.

This might be the toughest stretch of time to endure, because when the screws are turning a little tighter it can be almost impossible to maintain the level of concentration and output that your job requires. Continue to work hard, as best you can. Don't stop. And certainly, don't offer to quit.

If Eric's unsatisfactory conversation with his boss ends with her observation that he's clearly not happy in the company, Eric must respond:

"No, not at all. I've always loved my job. I haven't been unhappy here, but I am unhappy with the current circumstances. I've been paid to do a job, and I've done it well. I clearly added value to the organization. As I pointed out, however, I'm no longer included in important meetings, I have no salary increases, I have a great deal more work, and the lines of communication between us aren't functioning in a way that will enable me to do my work. As much as I would hate to think there's anything suspicious about this situation, this is a serious shift. And I am concerned."

Then Eric gets back to work and immediately sets in motion plans to obtain advice, either from internal or external sources or both.

Your first line of approach should be to see your HR professional. Ideally, you'll receive advice that you might need. (See the information on HR, page 29.) However, if their level of cooperation or support is not sufficient to make you feel more comfortable, there is nothing wrong with consulting an employment attorney, and it could be useful. This individual might be able to coach Eric on how to negotiate a severance package, if that's what he's after, or advise Eric on avoiding landmines that can involve a risk to his reputation in the job market.

• **Offer to negotiate.**

In the next level discussion with the boss, the goal is to present a diplomatic suggestion with both sides putting his and her cards on the table. As the employee functioning under this particular situation, you must convey the message that your job has changed so much that it's now a mission impossible.

For example, Eric might again approach his boss with the following comments:

"You've changed my job, while not rewarding me appropriately. Because the job has changed, I expect you to conform to that change with a promotion, a higher base salary, and an additional assistant to keep up with the work you're assigning me. An alternative possibility is that I be transferred to another department. Or, if I'm not going to be able to meet the requirements in my existing job, and a transfer is not possible, it seems to me that you need to help me exit this situation in a way that's a win for both of us. If you would like this position vacated, and because I believe it's a resource issue and not a matter of my performance, then I believe I deserve a decent severance package."

Ideally, you're offered a positive way to leave the organization. If not, it's definitely worth your while to consult an employment attorney.

All this could take a while. In the meantime, job hunt aggressively.

PART 4

SURVIVING DANGERS

A FEW FIRST THOUGHTS

Chapters 10 and 11—*The Immoral, Unethical, or Illegal Request* and *The Traumatic Event*—deal with surviving dangerous situations, the real killers that can have wide-reaching implications across the board, whether you are in a leadership position or not.

Mismanaging the unethical or illegal request or the traumatic event can have a powerful impact, and even devastating consequences, on individual lives and on the integrity of an organization as a whole. There is the possibility of increased risk to one's personal reputation or finances, the loss of personal freedom—possibly jail time—and/or the collapse of morale and productivity in the employee population.

10

THE IMMORAL, UNETHICAL, OR ILLEGAL REQUEST

HOW TO TELL IF YOU'RE RIGHT AND THEY'RE WRONG (OR A LITTLE OF BOTH)

They come down from bosses to underlings, these immoral, unethical, or illegal requests. They are among the thorniest, trickiest situations, involving as they do complex expectations or demands on multiple fronts—you, the individual employee; your boss; the organization; and, often, society in general in the form of laws and regulations.

Suppose you are asked to expedite a business donation to a boss's favorite charity that in no way complies with the company's policy guidelines for corporate contributions. This is a situation in which you know your supervisor is using company funds to further personal connections, and you are made to understand that your promotion rides on your compliance.

Suppose you're instructed to fire someone not on the grounds of performance but because your boss simply doesn't think that individual is young enough to do the job, and you're assigned to do the dirty work of finding a way to remove the employee from the organization. Or you're told to withhold relevant information from colleagues or to systematically demean a competitor's reputation, and you realize it's because of a boss's push for power or control. Or you are instructed to falsify information on a company report that will be in public records.

What do you do?

These requests run the gamut from treating people dishonestly or unfairly, to violating stated or implied ethical norms, to breaking the law. The consequences of obeying run the gamut as well, from feeling personally torn and upset, to taking part in a criminal activity. The consequences of *not* obeying can mean you end up off a career track or out of a job. Perhaps more than in any other tricky office situation, a careful due diligence of the external reality is crucial, and that might include learning about general corporate guidelines, a corporate ethical code spelled out in so many words, or, in fact, local, state, or federal regulations.

It's not a pleasant situation for anyone to be placed in, but some employees might have a particularly hard time. One sticking point relates to personality type or childhood experiences; the other has to do with more immediate issues of the day, such as the desperate need to hold on to a job.

We take a look at:

- The questionable request—and how employee Raoul coped
- The questionable request—and how employee Jenna coped.

Raoul's story: what happened to him one day on the job

"In some ways, I have great admiration for the man" said Raoul, 30, about his boss Lawrence. "He started out with virtually nothing, he put in 20-hour days, and he built this company that now employs over 100 people and does business in the millions every year." The company was an interior design and construction firm, with an emphasis on residential and commercial renovations in older buildings. Raoul called himself "Lawrence's right-hand man, gofer, sounding board, maitre d', general handyman. Lawrence can get high strung, I'm relatively laid back, so it's a good working collaboration in terms of personality." Raoul enjoyed the variety of the job, "no two days the same."

Occasionally, however, he had been bothered by his boss's tendency "to push the envelope, do things that I think are kind of questionable. He's basically decent, but maybe a little amoral. Or he goes for the expedient thing and just assumes there won't be any problems." A couple of times, the boss had given Raoul a directive that made Raoul uneasy. "Recently, for example, we needed to qualify by a deadline for submitting a contract in a bidding situation, and Lawrence left a message on my voice mail telling me to change the date on this letter of intent to the previous day and then notarize it. I didn't like that. I asked him about it." The boss, as had happened before, had what sounded like a sensible explanation—the document had been dictated on time, but the secretary hadn't prepared it until the following day. "Lawrence usually comes up with some reason why what he's asking me to do is okay, some kind of extenuating circumstances. Usually I see the point. And, of course, it's not like this happens on a daily basis."

He was a man without a firm set of values, maybe, Raoul thought, although not dishonest.

But one quality his boss displayed Raoul found distasteful, and that was his concern with how people looked. "We're in a business that's partly about appearances," Raoul said, "so I understand. But Lawrence has a bias against unattractive people; it's a real issue with him. Someone should look a certain way to be a good fit for the firm. He has strong reactions in this area." The bias was on display in an incident that left Raoul feeling backed into a corner. "Half a year ago we hired Stan, a designer who came with good credentials, good experience. He's had architectural training, a construction background. And he's performed above our expectations. The problem is, Stan is seriously overweight. He doesn't dress well. And Lawrence has been working up a head of steam about this guy, how he just doesn't go with the image of the place."

The boss wanted Stan out. He told Raoul to build a case of acceptable reasons to fire the man. "I think this is getting into dangerous territory," Raoul said. "Plus, I like Stan. I'm just delaying the whole business, putting off the inevitable." Sooner or later, however, he needed to address the particulars of the situation, including his own reluctance to meet it head on.

The internal reality piece: a diagnostic questionnaire

Some blind spots are likely to cause one to fret and fumble over how to proceed— even when *not* proceeding creates ever more stress and discomfort. Other blind spots can lead to rash behaviors that don't serve anyone well. So the questions are:

• Am I the obedient type?

A certain degree of obedience is expected from any employee, of course, but are you overly agreeable? Do you conform to authority—even if your conscience or common sense advises you not to—out of an unconscious need for affiliation and protection from the powerful parent/boss?

Do you fear the loss of love if you don't do what you're told?

Raoul categorized himself as not quite the blind conformist, not suffering from a fear of authority figures or a need for love. But he was "kind of a go-along type," he said. "I called myself laid back, but it's a little more complicated than that. I'm basically a 'yes' guy, I like to obey orders and keep the boss happy. But I won't let myself get pushed too far."

- **Am I tempted to storm the barricades at any hint of impropriety?**

Are you, we might say, something of a zealot?

The zealot is a sort of polar opposite to the conformist.

People who hold deeply felt convictions about right and wrong, who interpret the world as black or white, can be offended to the core by any request that seems a little grayish. This individual might have had a highly moralistic upbringing as a child; he knows what he knows. Faced with an office directive he doesn't like, he reacts fiercely and rejects it out of hand. Maybe he even threatens to expose the boss. Zealots are sometimes the angry whistle blowers in an organization.

The trouble is, storm the barricades at once, and you might not get at the truth or a sound business rationale for the request. When you refuse to honor a request because you pronounce it simply wrong, you allow for no flexibility and no dialogue. Not only then can you miss the truth; you might overreact badly and potentially burn your bridges with the people you report to.

The zealot believes only in his own interpretation of reality. But as the heading to this chapter suggested, sometimes it's not just that you're right and they're wrong, it's a little of both. Do you need to tone down a morally absolute stance and righteous indignation, in order to ask a few questions and obtain added perspective?

For example, consider Raoul and his boss's order that he pre-date and notarize the letter presenting the company's bid on a job. Raoul had a concern about that, he approached Lawrence with his concern, and he heard details that satisfied him—the letter had been delayed because of a mishap, the failure of the typist to prepare it on schedule. The request was perhaps on the borderline, but Raoul felt he could agree to it because his boss had no intention of doing something unethical.

The zealot provides no room for such an outcome.

Resist any urges toward the automatic "yes" or the automatic "no," so that you are able to discover a broader picture.

The external reality piece: a diagnostic questionnaire

Here's the main question:

• **Is my supervisor willing to engage in a dialogue?**

Is this individual someone who will help you get at the truth, if it's shaded in gray?

Someone who will listen to legitimate concerns or worries?

You might be working for a basically okay boss who is unlikely to ask you to do something knowingly and blatantly immoral, unethical, or illegal, but who has a somewhat free-wheeling or loose value system. Maybe he occasionally uses bad judgment. Maybe he's not too aware of society's rules and regulations or of the standards of conduct of the profession or particular organization. Perhaps, like Raoul's boss Lawrence, he's one who takes the expedient route, acts first and thinks later. Nevertheless, is he open to discussing the results of the request he's made? From your working history with this individual or from what you perceive of him as a human being, consider:

Is the boss available and willing to enter a two-way communication?

Can he handle constructive feedback?

Will he explain the reasons for his request? Is he capable of saying, "Well, yeah, this might be a little out of line, but here's why we're going to do it"?

If the answer is yes, you're in luck. Chances are you will be able to engage him in whatever way seems necessary, which might be outlining your personal objections or educating him about realities he hasn't considered.

If that's not the kind of person you're working for—if you sense or know for a fact there's no way you'd be able to voice your thoughts in a productive dialogue—here's where the lines of complexity cross.

How much are you able personally to obey a request that might be questionable though not illegal?

How much do you need the job? If a lot, what options do you have? We look at those issues in the scenario below, Jenna's story, but for now, what can Raoul do?

Best next steps

You might be dealing with an issue that is morally repugnant to you, or is against company ethical policy, or is just plain against the law. In any case, if you know you have a receptive boss and thus a good shot at dissuading him from the suggested course of action, give that a try. You don't want to antagonize this individual needlessly.

- **Present an alternative, the higher ground to take.**

Raoul made some initial suggestions to his boss, "putting off the inevitable," as he first perceived it. "We do have some high-end clients, and part of Stan's job is to do on-site consultations. So I suggested to Lawrence that we have Stan stay here in the shop, and not go out to the clients. That sounds terrible, like I'm saying nobody should have to see Stan, but I thought it was a way to handle some of Lawrence's issues, get me off the hook, and be fair to Stan, who's a good employee. Lawrence didn't go along with the idea, unfortunately."

If that doesn't work—the boss is not inclined to consider alternatives—time to ratchet up the argument. Convince him to share your concerns, whether they are over a flaunting of company policy or the possibility of running into legal problems in the future. This is the point at which, when dealing with an amoral or immoral but not evil boss, one who is ignorant or biased, it's necessary to educate and train him about the risks involved.

- **Stir up the boss's anxiety.**

Get the boss to be as anxious as you are. In a nonjudgmental, nonattacking way, convey the following message:

"I understand taking this action is what you require of me. I would like to, of course, because you're my boss, and I want to obey you, but I'm concerned about doing it, and I think you will be too once I remind you of some basic facts. Those are. . . ."

Talk about company policy that frowns on the action he's requested. Talk about concrete issues that might lead to trouble. So Raoul, for example, will tell boss Lawrence:

"You know, it's only acceptable to fire Stan if there's a performance problem. And there isn't one. He's been successful, and we really have no foundation for letting him go. I know you think he doesn't fit the company in terms of physical appearance, but he's doing a good job. We've had no complaints about him from our clients. So I'm very uncomfortable that if I go along with your request, we're at risk. For me to manufacture something against him, will open us both up to the potential for litigation. If Stan gets fired, he might hire a lawyer and sue the company."

What Raoul is communicating to his boss is the message: "I'm trying to protect us." And that should be the focus of this second-stage discussion—educate, train, communicate, be protective.

Ideally, all will go well; the boss will recognize the possibility of landing in hot water and change course. If all doesn't go well, consider the advice in Jenna's story.

Jenna's story: what happened to her one day on the job

Jenna, 26, was thrilled to land a job in the appraisal department of a major real estate firm, with offices in both the United States and Europe. Jenna's boss Abigail Elliott, a woman in her 50s, supervised her staff through a variety of assignments, including working with the insurance industry in arranging for property inspections, coordinating contracts with investment banks, and preparing reports for estate lawyers. What appealed to Jenna, she said, was "so much possibility to advance here. There are all kinds of directions I could move in eventually, including sales. And my boss is an encyclopedia of information and knowledge. She understands all aspects of the business."

Her own job so far was "largely bookkeeping—accounting work really. But by just being in the background, I'm picking up so much." Her boss was businesslike and not one to encourage familiarity. "The assistant I replaced told me the first day that I should always call the boss Mrs. Elliott, which gives our relationship a kind of formal feeling, but that's all right. She's started to hand me some interesting assignments, getting more into some of the appraisal researching. I see this as a sign she thinks I'm a good worker and she can trust me." Most of Jenna's day-to-day tasks still fell in the bookkeeping area, and that's where she ran into a problem.

One day her boss told Jenna to establish a new account into which certain paid receivables from clients would be deposited. She, Mrs. Elliott, would be the only person to access or have signature authority on that account and write checks against it, the boss told her assistant. "I was pretty sure that all the accounts had to have two signers," Jenna said, "There couldn't just be one person controlling the account. I told Mrs. E. that I thought it was company policy to have cosigners. She said I should just go ahead and do as she instructed."

Jenna felt both trapped and terrified. Trapped, because she was living from paycheck to paycheck, and wanted especially to hold on to this job. Terrified, because she realized immediately she was being asked to do something that might even lead to illegal activity. "It seemed to me that setting up this account the way she wanted could easily be laying the grounds for an embezzlement scheme."

She hadn't been in the job long enough to take a clear reading of her boss, though she was getting to know her as aloof, formal, "even somewhat secretive. She plays everything close to the vest." Feeling trapped and terrified was leading Jenna into paralysis.

The internal reality piece: a diagnostic questionnaire

• Is my need for a job dominating my vision?

This young woman was desperate to hold onto her job and her income. But a *bigger* goal for her had to be avoiding implication in a case of fraud. She needed to be very careful not to let her fear of being out of work blind her to the fact that she just possibly might become complicit in an illegal act and end up not being able to work anywhere. She needed to keep a clear eye on that worst-case scenario, which might not only cost her her job but damage her reputation in the industry.

• Am I tempted to dissemble?

Because you're afraid of getting on the boss's bad side, is your immediate instinct to sound acquiescent and make general noises suggesting you'll take care of the matter that has raised a red flag in your mind? This is a bad idea. You'll only dig yourself in deeper.

Don't lie. Don't say, "Okay, I'll do it," even though you're not intending to. To buy yourself a little time, the simplest response is probably to say, "I need to process your request a bit."

Control emotions that leave you feeling trapped or terrified, and at once begin to gather information.

The external reality piece: a diagnostic questionnaire

In response to the fallout from ethical and legal problems organizations have experienced in recent years, many companies have accelerated their displays of written codes of ethics and have developed in-house programs to support workers in stressful situations of this nature. Some such efforts have real bite; occasionally, they're essentially window dressing, with little impact. That doesn't mean you shouldn't try them. Due diligence begins with some fact finding.

• Is this an ethical organization in general?

When your boss has asked you to do something that's not clean, you might need help in extricating yourself from a potentially damaging situation. Can you expect to find it? Will the company support you?

Here's my bottom-line suggestion: The only surefire way to find out is to explore whether the organization rewards ethical behavior and disciplines unethical behavior, and whether the channels for employee concerns are not only safe, but have power to effect change. Frankly, to protect you. Ask around among colleagues—you need not say why you'd like to know.

Has a coworker had occasion ever to complain about unethical requests? Was she satisfied that her concerns were taken seriously? Were company assurances about keeping the whistle-blower's identity secret honored?

Have employees been disciplined for wrong behaviors in the past?

Best next steps

• Explain your reservations to the boss.

Let's say that Jenna decided she must face squarely the tricky situation she's in and she will not pretend she will take an action that worries her. Her next step will be determined by whether or not she feels her boss is capable of a two-way conversation and by whether or not she's threatened by her.

If the boss, Mrs. Elliott, is someone she believes she can talk to, she might say in a diplomatic tone:

"Of course, I would like to follow your request. You're my boss. But I can't do what you're asking. I believe we can't open a new account in the way you've outlined, because it's against company rules."

Suppose Mrs. Elliott responds that she still expects Jenna to set up the account. Jenna then says:

"I really will have to think about this. I'm uncomfortable. I'm afraid we can get into trouble."

At that point she must make a judgment call: Does Jenna tell the boss she will be talking to other people in the organization to obtain information and feedback? If she's really scared of her boss, feeling threatened, she might keep that plan to herself and just stick with "I have to think this over." Then she approaches the internal vehicles available to her for support.

The point is, once you tell your boss you're planning to talk to somebody else, you're raising *his* red flag. Quite possibly, you're about to get him into trouble. So proceed with care. When unethical people with power perceive a threat, their responses are not going to be restrained by the golden rule.

• Gather information.

Most large organizations have designated groups or individuals to whom an employee can turn for further information in these gray areas.

HR is one possibility. (See the information on HR, page 29.) Without necessarily revealing the whole story in detail, you might talk with your HR professional and find out what other internal avenues exist—who's the correct person to go to. You might be pointed in the direction of one of the following:

A "committee on good corporate practices" exists in some companies. The group might consist of a senior officer in charge of a code of ethics policy within the organization. This ombudsman and/or compliance officer will accept calls from employees who are facing requests to take immoral, unethical, or illegal actions, and can give advice in a confidential manner.

Many organization have ethics "hotlines," similar to the committee on good corporate practices though perhaps a bit less formal. You can call confidentially, outline what you're being asked to do, and inquire if it's right or wrong.

If your company has an employee assistance program, that might be a place to start. Again without going into great detail, simply say you've been asked to do something you believe is wrong, you need to know if you're over-reacting, and you'd like further information. The EAP representative might then call corporate practices on your behalf, and suggest that you'd like to have a confidential meeting to discuss the situation. (See the information on EAP, page 78.)

Finally, most large firms will have within the general counsel, or legal, department a compliance unit; in the controller's department there might be an audit division. In either, you might find a person you can talk to about unethical or illegal business related requests.

• Go to your boss's boss.

If the internal resources I've just outlined don't exist in your company, and you are not ready or are unable to consult an outside attorney, take your discussion to the next level in the chain of command. Go to your boss's boss, and being very specific, describe what you have been asked to do. This is the only chapter in this book in which I would encourage such a move. It's loaded with risk. Especially if your boss is unaware you will be taking this step, it can backfire on you.

Bringing your dilemma to any of these sources does involve a degree of risk. But when you are asked to cooperate in what you suspect is unethical, immoral, or illegal, the risk is preferable to the alternative.

11

THE TRAUMATIC EVENT

HOW TO BE AN INSPIRATIONAL CRISIS MANAGER (NOT AN OVERREACTING HERO OR AN UNDERREACTING MINIMIZER)

The traumatic workplace event is by no means common, certainly not on the order of the trigger scenarios we've looked at in previous chapters. It's hardly appropriate to lump this in the category of "tricky situations." Nevertheless, it is virtually impossible to live in this day and age without awareness that such events do happen and can have deleterious impact on a workforce. Few thoughtful individuals now feel truly immune to the threat of unexpected and devastating shocks.

Most profoundly, we have become unsettled, perhaps permanently, by the possibility of intentional acts of terrorism directed at unknown victims. Traumatic events can also include natural disasters such as hurricanes and earthquakes, and violence committed by an unstable citizen with grievances against a particular organization—the rare but horrifying story we hear on the nightly news of the disgruntled employee who returned to his former office with an automatic rifle. Corporate disasters brought on by inept, dishonest, or greedy management, where a once vital organization melts down in a relatively short period of time with employees losing jobs, life savings, and pensions, have also been much on our collective minds. On a smaller scale, the sudden death of a manager or popular coworker in an organization can reverberate painfully throughout the rest of the company.

Traumatic events tend to bring out the best or worst qualities in all of us—or more accurately, wise and useful or unwise and not useful responses to what has happened. However, unless we are soldiers trained for combat or uniformed officers or amazingly resilient people, most of us will react in a style we have learned during earlier points of crisis in our lives—perhaps in childhood—and which is further influenced by the emotional effects unique to the immediate time of trouble.

In this chapter—which is addressed to all employees in an organization, though especially to those in positions of management—I want to suggest some strategies that can ease everyone through the immediate aftermath of a traumatic event and set the stage for a process of rebirth and recovery. As you read them, you might find it useful to imagine a crisis situation affecting your particular company and work unit, and think through particular ways the suggestions might relate to you and your colleagues.

These are some of the priorities and coping behaviors to be considered in the event of a trauma or major workplace crisis.

The emotional needs of people must not be ignored

Some individuals respond effectively and at once to the many business consequences of a crisis, but overlook the human factor. These tend to be task-oriented people who work hard through the initial shock, keeping the system operating.

John, let's call him, a manager, has a powerful defensive strategy that enables him to downplay the emotional aftereffects of what has happened. He's a bit of a taskmaster who expects everyone to share his detached approach and snap back to work, as if nothing unsettling occurred. By denying the human element, not taking into account the psychological blow to his employees and not understanding their need for empathy and support, he misses the whole point.

John might be a perfectly kindhearted individual. But when overwhelmed, he copes with the fallout by repressing and denying his feelings, and he projects that onto others. He's an underreacting minimizer. Sometimes, on the other hand, the taskmaster by character or personality is simply a rather cold, insensitive person, who easily compartmentalizes his thoughts and behaviors between business and human relationships.

In a time of crisis, people are rattled. They're frightened. Morale, productivity, and loyalty can be decreased at a time when employees' motivation to function at peak performance is affected. The people, as well as the work, need attention.

Employees should feel empowered

Manager Mary, let's say, has the sensitivity and empathy that the taskmaster lacks, but goes beyond reasonable in her treatment of others, again due to personal defense mechanisms. She overcompensates out of a need to establish control over an uncontrollable event. Perhaps, irrationally, she believes she is guilty in some way. Perhaps she wants to feel like a hero, gathering everyone under her wing and making it all turn out okay. So Mary goes about taking care of those in her office, assuming all responsibilities herself. She's too protective. She treats her employees like children; she infantilizes individuals just at a time they themselves are struggling to regain a sense of their own powers to manage and structure the environment.

Individual strengths and vulnerabilities will be varied, but people do need to feel some sense of empowerment during the recovery process. The overreacting hero doesn't help.

Clear communication, as soon and as thorough as possible, is essential

Confusion and overwhelming anxiety is usually the initial response to a traumatic event—when facts aren't apparent, when consequences are largely unknown, and when strategies for future steps are vague. The key to beginning recovery and reducing anxiety is quick, direct, candid, straightforward communication that provides some semblance of clarity and, at the same time, appreciation for what everyone is going through. People in the organization need to receive information about objectives, roles, and responsibilities. They want demonstration of concern for the welfare of staff and their families. They want to know that work environments will provide some stability in the immediate future.

It's critical that employees and managers communicate in whatever technology is available to ensure that everyone is on message, even if it requires going over the same information again and again. In some situations, when management is distracted or in denial or just not functioning adequately, individual employees might need to take on leadership roles temporarily to fill the void and make sure necessary information is disseminated. Those tasks might involve simply contacting everyone and arranging for an off-site location to meet.

Posttraumatic confusion and anxiety usually last for at least a month. The sooner individuals get information, some semblance of stability, and sources of empathy, the quicker the recovery process will get underway.

Routine resources should be established

One of the most visible consequences in the aftermath of a major crisis is a disruption in regular ways of working. Alternative solutions, with the help of management, might need to be put into place. If an office building is damaged and temporarily unlivable, for example, perhaps a group of employees can work out of one colleague's apartment for a time.

Recognizable routines, as much as they can be established, help promote resilience and a feeling of safety.

Individual counseling or group support programs can be invaluable

Almost everyone will experience emotional distress, at least within the first month. This can be a crazy time. Even basically sturdy people sometimes react in ways that are unfamiliar; they don't recognize themselves; they've never seen themselves behave in these ways before. That's a normal reaction to a shockingly abnormal situation, a temporary setback.

It's wise to assume that everyone with be distressed to some degree, regardless of individual differences and of the extensiveness of the trauma. Employee assistance personnel, corporate-sponsored counselors, and other support programs should be in place, with individuals encouraged to participate in such help efforts. Such support is a good arena in which people can express their fears, pessimistic thoughts, and other negativity without burdening others.

Some employees might be overwhelmed. This person's behavior on the job is severely disrupted because of the impact of the trauma on her personal life. She might be rendered paralyzed and impotent in handling work responsibilities, really unable to perform or lead, especially during the early stages of recovery. Such individuals can't help themselves without outside intervention, and might need additional recuperation time.

Personal and family maintenance is critical

Every employee of an organization really needs to make sure that he and his family members get the necessities of life—sleep, food, a stable home—while recovering from a major crisis. This is no time to be hesitant or embarrassed about seeking and accepting all available governmental, nonprofit, corporate, or religious support.

Relentless preparation is essential

Organizations and individual employees are morally obliged, it seems to me, to be as prepared as possible for worst-case scenarios in the workplace. For management, that calls for relentless preparation for developing strategic plans that involve all corporate support efforts, including accurate record retention and retrieval procedures, up-to-date employee and family contact information, emergency evacuation instructions and rehearsals, and back to work services for employees. For individuals, it means paying serious attention to corporate policies, prepping family members on ways to keep in touch during a time of confusion, maintaining up-to-date personal documents (birth certificates, insurance information, passports, medical records and the like) in an easily accessible place, and understanding some of the key ingredients of personal resiliency.

12

BEYOND TODAY

SURVIVAL STRATEGIES FOR STAYING SANE WHILE TAMING TIGERS AT WORK

After more than 30 years as a counselor and coach, I have targeted the most mature, most realistic survival strategies that will help anyone maintain emotional stability and personal effectiveness through the multiple trigger situations that arise in work organizations. Some of my strategies are, frankly, quite easy. Some are more difficult. However, all demand planning and a determination to follow through and stick with it. They lead to the kind of healthy and adaptive defenses, attitudes, and actions that are, ultimately, self-protective and empowering.

Here, now, is a recap and a few final suggestions.

Commit to becoming and remaining self-aware

Which work situations trigger your vulnerabilities?

Throughout this book you have read a sampling of on-the-job troublesome scenarios, but almost certainly there are others we did not highlight and to which you might be particularly sensitive. Tune in to your triggers. Identify the feelings, thoughts, and behaviors they typically provoke in you. Try to reflect on where those patterns have originated and what the triggers might symbolize.

Knowing your blind spots is the key to not letting yourself get blindsided.

Control negative emotions

Unmanaged negative feelings can lead automatically to negative thinking and to inappropriate behaviors that are not adaptive to the situation you're in.

Something happens on the job that causes you to feel enraged, sad, or fearful. Those emotions are real to you. They should not be denied. Acknowledge them to yourself, as at the same time you attempt to link them to external triggers. But most importantly, do not act impulsively.

In the previous chapters, you've read some strategies that can be useful when you're caught up in overwhelming emotions and need to get a grip, in order to figure out your best next steps. There are no absolute magical solutions; no one size fits all; there might be a different answer for everyone and for every situation. Do what works for you.

For example:

Safely vent through talks with helpful friends and professionals.

Engage in relaxation techniques, such as meditation or deep breathing.

Engage in physical exercise, a most effective way of exorcising emotional demons.

Leave the immediate scene. Let's say you're in a meeting with coworkers, information is being inaccurately or unfairly presented, you're aware your heart is racing and your fists are clenching in anger, but you can't in the moment think clearly enough to process your feelings and convert them into an appropriate action. Get out of there. Exit—even if you have to employ a ruse to do so. One of my clients, understanding explosive anger as an issue for him, kept his cell phone in his pocket on vibrator. When in a situation that prompted him to react impulsively, he indicated that his cell phone vibrator had signaled—of course, no one else knew—and excused himself to return the pretended phone call. This was, frankly, a white lie that enabled him to leave the scene and give himself time to calm down.

If you experience especially acute and powerful emotional reactions that are hard to control through these various methods, a consultation with a mental health professional is in order. Often, a psychopharmacologist is recommended when a medication approach is desirable in reducing the impact of your emotions. Some people claim that homeopathic, natural remedies might also impact anxiety.

However you do it, protect your attitude and your actions from the negative feelings that have been promoted. Do not react impulsively

Think adaptively

That is, develop an outlook of optimism and belief in your ability to handle the stressful dilemmas you might be facing.

Creating this mindset takes practice, because distracting emotions can so easily get in the way of a rational, positive approach. Fortune cookie wisdom is instructive here: "The winner knows he's a winner from the beginning. The loser is even more certain of his fate, and they're both right." People who look sad, angry, or frightened, whose talk radiates pessimism, who wallow in self pity are likely to build up greater than average real justification for their poor results. Aim for a self-fulfilling prophecy: believe you will navigate the turbulent waters and you will. Some positive techniques can help:

Practice reframing. Reframing is a cognitive technique the goal of which is to find something good in a bad or stressful situation. Rather than focusing on what's wrong or what you have lost, figure out what you can learn or gain. It's truly like turning lemons into lemonade. For example: Instead of ruminating on how crazy your boss makes you, think about what an interesting opportunity you have to practice developing strong defenses when dealing with difficult people, and how helpful that will be in multiple other situations that you'll no doubt face sooner or later.

Practice positive self talk. A related cousin of reframing, this process is a little more concrete. It entails interrupting the specific negative thoughts occupying your mind, trying to force them out of your consciousness, and replacing them with optimistic, pleasant ones. If you find yourself obsessing about how irritating your boss's actions were that morning, distract yourself immediately. Think about how much you're looking forward to going home tonight and having a great dinner with your spouse or playing with your child, or what movie you're planning to see. Recognize the negative flow of thought and turn it off, especially if you're not using those thoughts for constructive solutions.

Maintain good shock absorbers

Good shock absorbers come in two forms, the financial and the personal. So:

Be thrifty. Being thrifty is being smart. Don't spend all the money you earn. Try to establish savings and create some liquid money in the bank in order to achieve a financial cushion. If you know you have six months' salary in reserve, it's a psychological insurance policy. When you're feeling trapped, when you believe you want to or must leave your job, that cushion helps you see your way out of an impossible situation. And if you decide not to leave after all, there's magic in compounding!

Create and maintain a wide network of professional colleagues and mentors for career purposes, and a small cabinet of trusted advisors, which might include a career counselor, an executive coach, a mental health professional, or an employment attorney. Even if you never need to seek out their services, either in the present or the future, identifying these individuals as good references and having them in your contact file can itself be extremely anxiety relieving. Simply keeping a list of names and numbers of useful people to contact will make you feel more confident, more hopeful, and better able to weather a toxic time.

At all costs, avoid or set limits on negative, whiney people in any of your networks, those who offer poor advice or are consistently pessimistic. Like the flu, negative people are contagious. They might unintentionally encourage you to indulge in self-pity or rage; they are apt to increase rather than decrease the impact of your blind spots.

Make sure that those friends, colleagues, or professionals you reach out to for support have the empathy, the trustworthiness, and the smarts to offer true value. Especially if you know that you will be looking for another job, get yourself a cheerleading squad. These supportive people can be positive mirrors to you, and reinforce your value at a time you need confirmation that you're okay. And you are.

Embrace change

Try to knock down any remaining resistance you might have to the new, the different, and the evolving. Commit yourself to being out in front of the curve so you don't find yourself behind it. Probably the biggest obstacle blocking career progress is fear of change.

But please don't wait for a crisis on your job or for management-imposed orders to get you motivated. Be proactive. If you can, seek out the training, education, or information on the latest trends in your particular area of expertise. Read books, read magazines, or attend professional meetings. Take advantage of company-sponsored offerings.

Volunteer for development, training, or executive coaching programs in which you work on adopting new skills and broadening your leadership capabilities.

It's important to be prepared. At the least, you will be protecting yourself from becoming a victim of the status quo and from feeling overwhelmed by external pressures as they arrive.

Develop the skill of detachment

As much as possible, keep your ego separate from your organizational persona. I know it's hard. But the criteria for rewards on the job might be politically driven, unfair, and irrational at times. You really can't take it personally. Remember that an organization is not a family; you are not its child; bad stuff can happen, even though you don't deserve it. However, bad stuff happening on the job is not the same as being unloved or abandoned by family and important others in your life.

I like to think of this skill as developing a psychological protective coating to help you get through the rough patches. One way to protect yourself and have some of your psychological needs met is to make a real effort to find sources of self-esteem outside the work environment—in your family, your community, your professional associations, your hobbies. Away from the job, take up yoga, take up tai chi, go jogging or fast walking, meet with friends, develop a book club, do volunteer work.

Communicate artfully

Sooner or later, you almost surely will find yourself in an office dilemma in which you hope to convey constructive feedback—to a boss, a coworker, or a subordinate. You wish to encourage that individual to modify his behavior. It's crucial, then, to learn the skill of disarming and diffusing another's defensiveness when the two of you are head-to-head in a tricky situation.

If you approach such a conversation by confronting your colleague about bad or incorrect behavior, you're more than likely to increase his tension, conflict, and resistance. He feels attacked and judged; certainly he's probably not motivated to see the error of his ways and do better. On the other hand, start by commenting on something positive—good work he's done before, accomplishment in his area of expertise—and he feels valued, to some degree anyway. If possible, too, take him off the hook by assuming that his negative behavior is unintentional.

Be diplomatic. Communicate artfully. Unless he's the destructive type we've talked about earlier, your respectful manner will more than likely decrease his defensiveness and lead to improvements.

Communicate with discretion

On the job, be super careful what you say and how you say it.

First, the matter of office gossip:

Gossip is a natural human behavior. It's a stress reliever, it can be fun, and people enjoy it. But making a habit of it is not a good idea. Telling tales on others can show disrespect and questionable ethics; in addition, it can return to haunt and damage you.

When you're gossiping about people you work with—their character, their incompetence, or their personal problems—be extraordinarily cautious, even when talking to people you trust. Especially in times of organizational stress, when individuals are vying for positions or frightened for their jobs, coworkers who formerly were your buddies might end up using information against you. You don't want to make yourself vulnerable to the possibility of others thinking you slandered them by sharing information or opinions about their personal lives.

Potentially, gossiping around the office water cooler or microwave is like talking to the *New York Times*. There is a high risk factor that such talk will come out and hurt you and make you appear unethical.

Second, the matter of e-mails and voice mails:

Some of the worst political mistakes I have encountered among my clients or their colleagues have involved the discovery of indiscreet, rageful, or impulsive office e-mail or voice mail messages. One man was having an affair with a coworker, sending her sexual notes and poems on her computer. In some way, these communications were uncovered by management, the participants were embarrassed and compromised, and one had to leave the firm. Some employees wrote e-mails to staff or to the boss while at the height of anger, with unfortunate consequences. Even more than a telephone voice mail, an e-mail that conveys a hostile message has an enormously negative impact. A flip or aggressive or rude one-liner is so much more hurtful or disrespectful than any face-to-face conversation about problems, when words can be buffered by personal contact.

E-mail has no face and no tone or nuance. Even though voice mail has a tone, adding a little human factor, anger or disrespect can still easily be conveyed. When using these communication vehicles to vent annoyance or give uncomfortable feedback, be extraordinarily careful at least to balance your message with some expression of respect. Begin with the positive, whatever you can find. For example, let your e-mail say: "I know it's been a stressful time, I know you're just back from maternity leave, I'm aware that you're overloaded right now, I appreciate that, but we need to talk about the consequences of XYZ, because it's becoming a problem. Get back to me as soon as you can." That's a lot better than: "You screwed up, I'm furious, see me immediately."

Remember that everyone is a customer

In my coaching practice, I have found it extremely useful to advise my corporate clients to view all the significant people in their work environment—subordinates, peers, boss—as customers. Somehow, mentally placing people in that context prompts you naturally to think more carefully about their needs than you otherwise would. You almost automatically become more empathetic, which in turn helps you to adapt your behaviors to better fit and manage their concerns.

An empathetic posture always aids in creating goodwill and in skirting conflict.

Avoid the fundamental attribution error

You've had one bad encounter with an office colleague. And now and forever more you're tempted to chalk her up as an all-around, personally bad individual—forgetting that her actions might have been at least partially attributable to an array of other factors.

Try not to do that. Give others a second and maybe a third chance, and then conduct your due diligence along the lines I've suggested in previous chapters. With careful observation and in time, you'll probably be able to determine whether her bad behavior was a temporary blip or an indication of a consistent character shortcoming or flaw.

Take responsibility for staying fit and in good health

It's no surprise that a physically fit and mentally alert person is better equipped with the stamina and heartiness needed to cope with the stresses of organizational life than one who isn't fit and alert. So make it your business to maintain good habits regarding nutrition, exercise, and relaxation. Obviously, we can't control all the vicissitudes that life throws at us, but enough evidence has demonstrated that adhering to a healthful and balanced lifestyle can greatly enhance the immune system and is a good defense against disease.

It's especially important to nurture yourself. Focused so fixedly on jobs, income, and success as we tend to be, it's easy to forget about seeking out pleasure and relaxation. In a busy world, even exercise becomes work. There's little time left to truly unwind. I encourage the habit of finding buffer zones in the day, the evening, and the weekend, whether it's in the form of a regularly scheduled massage, or reading a novel, or taking a nap, or arranging for a girls' night out or a boys' night out or a romantic evening with a spouse—something that doesn't involve achievement, but restores energy balance.

Seek professional assistance when necessary

Sometimes self-awareness, willpower, logic, stamina, good friends, money in the bank, all that might not be enough permanently and consistently to get control over a blind spot, the feelings it creates, and the vulnerabilities it produces on the job. When workplace demands trigger those emotions and behaviors on a regular basis, again and again, it really might be necessary and wise to consult a trained professional.

If your feelings are chronic and disruptive, consider consulting a mental health professional to determine an approach that would be most effective, which might be therapeutic intervention—talk therapy—with a possible supplementary support such as anxiety reducing or other medications. That can become an invaluable source of support while you're trying to change old patterns and responses.

Rehearse for your next gig

Don't wait to be downsized or to quit in order for you to think about your next career move. Even if you're comfortable in your present position, there's nothing wrong, but actually a lot right, with periodically reflecting on your skills and interests and on the marketplace in general. Develop other scenarios of what you might be doing if you didn't have the job you have now.

Sometimes it's helpful to see yourself as a skill merchant,

someone who can actually go out and sell a particular expertise. Could you become a consultant in your specialty? If you remain a corporate citizen, in what other industry might you apply your knowledge, talents, and experience? A little rehearsing along these lines can be conducted on your own or in consultation with a career counselor. Either way, assessing options is a good proactive plan and a good move. If something bad does happen—if you're suddenly out of a job—it can take three to six months or more to go through the process of resettling. Don't start from ground zero.

Adjust your value system

Let it reflect the reality of the marketplace.

At the end of the day, we really don't have ultimate control over the rewards to be garnered from doing a good job. And if you base your value system and esteem solely on achievement, success, and material returns, you're potentially priming yourself to feel either that you have failed or that something is missing in your world.

In my experience, if you can add into your value system as you get older a philosophy of life that incorporates the importance of spiritual values—meaning, purpose, love—that can sustain you when you're going through tough times at work. When you feel your talents and efforts are not sufficiently recognized and rewarded by the marketplace, those values can go a long way towards alleviating your disappointments.

Periodically evaluate the fit between you and your job

If you are constantly stressed and unhappy at work, if you feel in conflict with the culture in which you find yourself, then act *as if* you fit and take care of the effects privately—physical exercise, good friendships, hobbies, and so on.

If you are constantly stressed and unhappy, revise your concept of success: Instead of wanting to be singled out and rewarded for your achievement of specific work goals, perhaps you can decide it's enough to be perceived as a comfortable piece of the organizational puzzle, whatever that might mean in your organization.

If none of that works, leave.

There might come a time when you decide you must seek out a healthier work environment and a better fit. If you consider yourself a dynamo who thrives on risk-taking, for example, but work within a conservative company that doesn't take kindly to such behavior, you'll probably not do well—and probably never be happy where you are. Find the corporate culture that suits you. Resolve to be happier at work. Why shouldn't you be?

These might not be all the survival strategies that are out there. They are some I have found to be the most helpful. Here's an extra bonus: In learning and practicing what you need to know about success in the workplace—recognizing triggers, managing emotions, doing your due diligence, thinking through solutions—you're not only helping yourself on a day-to-day basis at work, but you are developing resiliency and a coping strategy for life in general. Rely on them in other difficult life situations as well, when you wish to survive and thrive.

Index

Photo by Ezequiel De La Rosa

ABOUT THE AUTHORS

Marilyn Puder-York, Ph.D., is a clinical psychologist and a former vice president who led an in-house global employee assistance program in a Fortune 500 company. A pioneer is applying clinical psychology to the enhancement of careers, Dr. Puder-York for more than 25 years has helped employees identify and manage their internal barriers in order to achieve superior performance, currently in her work as a corporate sponsored coach of senior executives. She is a member of the Human Resource Planning Society and the American Psychological Association, and a fellow of the New York Academy of Medicine. She lives in Connecticut with her husband and daughter.

A New York based freelance writer and former magazine editor, **Andrea Thompson** has cowritten many books in the areas of psychology, parenting, and human relations.